Mastering Work Intake
From Chaos to Predictable Delivery

Thomas M. Cagley, Jr.
SAFe® Practice Consultant (SPC)
Certified Scrum Master (CSM)

and

Jeremy Willets
SAFe® Practice Consultant (SPC)

Copyright © 2024 by Thomas M. Cagley, Jr. and Jeremy Willets

ISBN-13: 978-1-60427-200-0

Printed and bound in the U.S.A. Printed on acid-free paper.

10 9 8 7 6 5 4 3 2 1

The Library of Congress Cataloging-in-Publication Data can be found on the WAV section of the publisher's website at www.jrosspub.com/wav.

Phone: (954) 727-9333
Fax: (561) 892-0700
Web: www.jrosspub.com

To my wife, Barb:

Thank you for putting up with me and my obsession with trying to make the world a better place. Oh, and the dad jokes.

—Tom

To Corinne, Cecilia, and Cordelia:

Thank you for your never-ending support on this journey.

—Jeremy (Dad)

CONTENTS

ABOUT THE AUTHORS

Thomas M. Cagley, Jr., is a consultant, speaker, author, coach, and agile guide who leads organizations and teams to unlock their inherent greatness. He has developed estimation models and has supported organizations developing classic and agile estimates. Tom helps teams and organizations improve cycle time, productivity, quality, morale, and customer satisfaction, and then prove it.

Tom is an internationally respected blogger and podcaster for over 11 years, focusing on software processes and measurement. His blog entries and podcasts have been listened to or read over a million times. He coauthored *Mastering Software Project Management: Best Practices, Tools and Techniques* with Murali K. Chemuturi. Tom penned the "Agile Estimation Using Functional Metrics" chapter in *The IFPUG Guide to IT and Software Measurement*. His certifications include SAFe® Practice Consultant (SPC) and Certified Scrum Master (CSM).

More information about Tom can be found at tomcagley.com.

Jeremy Willets is a coach, speaker, and author who has spent the last decade working with people and teams to achieve greatness in the workplace. He started out as a technical writer on a Scrum team and quickly fell in love with Scrum and the Agile Manifesto values and principles. Since then, he's served thriving organizations as a Scrum Master, agile coach, senior agile coach, release train engineer, people manager, and mentor.

Jeremy has spoken at conferences throughout the midwestern United States. He's an avid Substack blogger and music maker. He holds the SAFe® Practice Consultant (SPC) certification.

More information about Jeremy can be found at jeremywillets.com.

PREFACE

WHY WORK INTAKE?

Regardless of whether you're creating, enhancing, or maintaining products, work intake is a challenge you will deal with. Those who choose to ignore it run the risk of a semipermanent state of thrashing. This is the same as chasing the proverbial new shiny object instead of doing the thing that customers will actually pay you for. Mastering work intake could very well make or break your career and your company. It is the only path from chaos to predictability.

When we thought about the idea of writing a book on this topic, we did our research. It was shocking that such a small number of texts deal with this topic. Many focus on what to do when the work is in progress or the mechanics of work prioritization. But very few focus on the full pipeline that work follows as it enters and exits your system. They also ignore the fact that different types of work enter at different levels and times. The unwillingness to tackle work intake is one of our industry's dirty little secrets.

We have worked with great engineering teams and organizations that experienced work intake challenges. They ended up either building the wrong thing or building the right thing, but at the wrong time. In all cases, there were significant ramifications—it was chaos. Across the industry, work intake is still a problem. The reasons for this are many, and we'll explore many of those antipatterns in this book.

Here is a final word as to why we chose this topic: poor work intake frustrates everyone—including customers and coworkers. We hope this book will help everyone in the world of product development feel a lot less frustration and at least a little more satisfaction with their work.

THIS BOOK IS FOR YOU

At one time or another, work intake has been a common challenge for every software team that we have worked with. Here are our thoughts on how this work will be useful to you:

- **Agile coach/Scrum Master:** We have spent most of our careers in these roles, and this material is definitely written from that perspective. Scrum Masters and agile coaches help teams as they face decisions concerning what to work on. These are often difficult questions. Expect to see examples of antipatterns throughout, as well as the steps we took to resolve them.
- **Product owner/product manager:** Prioritization of work is an important work intake concept. It is fundamental to the product owner and product manager roles. We will explore many strategies that you can use when prioritizing. These strategies will be especially useful when everyone wants a different thing or if you are working in an organization without the capacity to execute the main business needs.
- **Portfolio epic sponsor:** If this is your role, you're making large commitments on behalf of your company. We will explore how to make these commitments consistent and repeatable.
- **Portfolio manager:** This role facilitates the refinement and prioritization of higher level backlog items. The goal is to link them up to business objectives. There must be a relationship between organizational goals and each team's stories. If there is no relationship, strategy and innovation will suffer.
- **Project manager/program manager:** These roles care about whether teams or programs are working on the right things

at the right time. Executing work in flight is part of mastering work intake.

- **Team member:** The team that is creating the product plays a critical role in the development of the product. These roles are more than coming in and writing or testing code for eight hours every weekday. Being a team member demands that you remain cognizant of priorities as you are working. You must also exercise discipline when work enters the team. How can team members influence the trajectory of the work they do, as well as the organization? Mastering work intake involves recognizing that it's easy to say "yes" and much harder to say "no."

- **Manager/team lead:** People leaders at the team level have a part to play in the work intake equation. You need to know what your team is executing on, what work is next, and the skill sets required to do the work. The work in front of your team might be a perfect match for their skill sets right now, but there are always opportunities for professional development.

- **Director/senior manager:** People leaders at a higher level have an economy of scale to worry about when it comes to work intake. Engineering organization leaders want to understand how the business is using engineering capacity. These leaders want their people to execute a company-wide strategy and product vision. Visualization and measurement are crucial work intake concepts to understand and practice.

- **Executive/sponsor (C-level, VP-level):** People at this level are making large commitments on behalf of their organizations. For example, a conversation with a customer at a trade show may lead to an idea for a product enhancement. It's great to have the organizational clout to be able to fast-track requests. But what's the actual cost of expediting something? There are ramifications for accepting new work into any system. Just because you have a big stick doesn't mean you should swing it all the time.

- **Customer-facing internal stakeholder:** People in sales, tech support, etc., often spend time engaging with customers. These roles have first-hand experience and visibility into customer challenges and requests. They have better insight into how the products are being used than the teams who are developing them. When it is time to prioritize work, how can you use this knowledge to make sure that the rest of the company listens to you?

- **Customer:** Last, but never least, we all use software products daily. We are all customers and we all have ideas on how to improve the products that we use. What happens, though, when product development happens without customer input? We'll discuss strategies you can use as a customer to get your voice heard.

This list of roles isn't comprehensive, but we are hopeful that it gives you a sense of the value of this material, regardless of which type of role you occupy. We had a great time putting this book together. But we know that this book won't be successful unless it provides significant value to readers and practitioners.

IS THIS AN AGILE BOOK?

We've spent many years working with agile teams and organizations. We've also spent a lot of time working in contexts that aren't using agile. While we wrote with an agile lens, this book applies to most business operating systems. Regardless of how a business creates and supports products, work is going to enter the system. If you don't get this right, you won't be in business for very long.

Traditional project management methods are still thriving in many firms. If this is your company, congratulations! You have a huge opportunity to impact how your company creates and supports products. We're confident that you'll find ideas in this book to try out. And remember, *being agile* is not the goal, per se; the goal is flexibility in how you bring products to market. Mastering work intake is a main tenet in reclaiming flexibility for your company.

HOW TO USE THIS BOOK

This book combines theory and experience to diagnose and solve work intake problems. All chapters include *Learning Objectives* and *End-of-Chapter Questions*. Many chapters include a variety of callouts:

- **You Asked:** answers to common questions. The explanation picks up where the theory in the text ends and adds greater context so you can apply the new ideas.
- **Experience Report:** an example of a real-world situation. Drawn from our experiences or interviews with practitioners to highlight the topic.
- **Experiment:** example of how to diagnose an issue and to help you address the topic. Experiments include proposed problem statements, hypotheses, how to validate your outcomes, and an example.

FINAL THOUGHTS ON WORK INTAKE AND AGILE

The *Agile Manifesto* was a rebellious act. It attacked the outdated methods used to create software products at the time. Waterfall was chief among them. The authors of this book have very different pedigrees. Jeremy never had the pleasure of working in a waterfall environment, while Tom has. Regardless, both can picture work intake in that context. The picture in Jeremy's mind goes something like this:

Your team is working on a project with different stage-gate phases. The developers finished writing the code based on a 100-page specification document. Everything is committed to a customer by a certain date. Everyone has signed off on the document, even though most only skimmed it. The testers have begun the testing phase. You expect that the developers will spend the next two months fixing the bugs that the testers find. Then, your team will prepare the project for deployment.

Yesterday, a product manager asked you whether the team could do a new piece of high-priority work. They said it's going to be "pretty big." You have a choice to make. You can interrupt the team with this new work or wait until they are completely done. Your choice is disruption or a long lead time for a new high-priority request. You seem to have very little flexibility.

When we discussed this scenario, Tom shook his head and laughed. Phrases like "We will get to that in phase two" and "Who's in for working all weekend?" were not jokes. They were—and are—the reality of the situation facing development teams.

Unfortunately, this reality rings true today. Work entering during a sprint or between planning events is common. When new work appears, saying "no" seems counter to continuous value delivery. Saying "yes" to new work is exactly the opposite, though. It crushes the continuous delivery of anything and is antithetical to being agile. Flexibility on behalf of customers is important, but it only matters if you actually deliver the right value when needed. Mastering work intake is the capability that will actually deliver what is needed when it is needed.

ACKNOWLEDGMENTS

This book is the result of nearly three years' worth of iterative and incremental progress. It is the result of hundreds of hours spent writing and editing in the early hours of the morning, in the lobby while waiting for kids to finish lessons, or at the end of a long day when everyone else at home was already asleep. This work is also the result of hundreds of hours of collaborative Zoom calls with each other.

We could not have produced this work on our own. We would like to thank Barb Cagley, who reformatted all the illustrations in the home stretch of creating this work. We would also like to thank the people who answered our call to review some (or all) of this work: Linda Podder, Benjamin Woznicki, Melissa Greller, Jillian Testa, Ryan Sylvester, and David Herron. We are grateful for the time they dedicated to giving us feedback. We are even more grateful to call them friends.

We would like to thank Stephen Buda at J. Ross Publishing. His expert guidance throughout the publishing process was greatly appreciated.

Finally, we'd like to acknowledge the people whose work has inspired us to write on this topic: Jim Benson, Daniel Vacanti, Donald Reinertsen, Johanna Rothman, Mik Kersten, and W. Edwards Deming. Their work has changed us—and it has changed the world.

INTRODUCTION TO TERMS

We will define lots of terminology throughout this book, but here are a few general terms that will not be explained in the text:

- *Agile*: the agile software development movement, which began in the early 2000s.
- *Agile Manifesto*: the document created by a conclave of software industry veterans at a ski resort in Utah. You can read the manifesto at https://agilemanifesto.org.
- *Scrum*: the framework for product development that was popularized by Jeff Sutherland and Ken Schwaber. You can read the Scrum Guide at https://www.scrum.org.
- *Kanban*: the lean method of visualizing work and managing work in progress. It was popularized in the world of software by people like David Anderson and Jim Benson.
- *Scaled Agile Framework* (SAFe®): the Scaled Agile Framework bills itself as the leading system for scaling agile. You can read about the framework at https://www.scaledagileframework.com/.
- *Product development*: the act of developing products. In this work, we will focus on product development in the software realm.
- *Extreme programming* (XP): Extreme programming is one of several popular agile processes. You can read more at http://www.extremeprogramming.org.

- *Program*: the Project Management Institute (PMI) defines a program as "a group of related projects managed in a coordinated way to obtain benefits and control not available from managing them individually."* We will use this definition throughout this text. For more information about how PMI defines a *program* and distinguishes it from a *project*, see https://www.pmi.org/le arning/library/understanding-difference-programs-versus-pro jects-6896.

---

* "Program Management." Project Management Institute, 7/22/2023, www.pmi.org/ learning/featured-topics/program.

At J. Ross Publishing we are committed to providing today's professional with practical, hands-on tools that enhance the learning experience and give readers an opportunity to apply what they have learned. That is why we offer free ancillary materials available for download on this book and all participating Web Added Value™ publications. These online resources may include interactive versions of the material that appears in the book or supplemental templates, worksheets, models, plans, case studies, proposals, spreadsheets and assessment tools, among other things. Whenever you see the WAV™ symbol in any of our publications, it means bonus materials accompany the book and are available from the Web Added Value Download Resource Center at www.jrosspub.com.

Downloads for *Mastering Work Intake* include facilitated exercises to help you formulate ideas to address work intake challenges in your context and instructional material for classroom use (lecture slides, exercise solutions, etc.).

Section One

Section One

Work Intake

Section Contents

SECTION INTRODUCTION

The way in which work gets to an organization or team isn't often discussed in polite company. Have you ever heard of a conference on work intake? Or even a track at a conference? The topic is either viewed as "boring," "the way it has to be," or so far "out of control" that it's not worth discussing. Those are excuses and rationalizations. When work intake comes up, it's generally couched in soft terms. These terms give the work intake process a nice, dull appearance. They obscure the importance of mastering work intake. It's the largest determinant of whether an organization or team can get work done.

We previewed the content of this book to a group of trusted colleagues and friends. At the time, we were using *work entry* to describe work intake. One of the feedback comments we received was, "Don't you mean work intake?" The short answer was, "No." The path to that simple answer is a bit longer.

Understanding why we thought *entry* was the correct term for this book is important. *How work gets done* is a building block toward understanding agile, lean, or waterfall principles. True agile and lean teams pull prioritized work based on capacity and capabilities. They do this rather than the alternative, which is having work pushed on them. More traditional approaches, such as those embodying the Capability Maturity Model Integration best practices, are more push-oriented, although they do consider team and organizational capacity and capabilities. Regardless of approach, process and practice are only somewhat related.

Intake refers to both *how* the work is acquired and the *amount of work* taken into a team or organization. The word *take* implies that the team or organization has the power to accept (or pull) the work. The idea of intake requires teams to have a real choice. Pulling work based on capacity that is determined via planning is an example of choice. Other examples of choice include planning work based on a Monte Carlo simulation or yesterday's weather. When teams live by lean and agile principles, their process for getting work is *intake*.

Embracing the more abrasive term *work entry* was a journey. It crystallized while Tom was re-reading the book *Coaching Agile Teams* by Lyssa Adkins. In Chapter 3 of that seminal work, Adkins discusses the impact of violent language. For coaches, language correlates to impact. In our estimation, *intake* is a softer, more neutral word than *entry*. Our intent has never been to write about this topic in a neutral manner. This is because that tone rarely matches our experiences with the topic.

Entry is forceful and aggressive; it implies pushed work. Regardless of professed philosophy, when work is *pushed*, the term *intake* sugarcoats problems. The word *entry* does not. Pushed or uncontrolled acceptance of work is not agile. If a team or organization cannot control how they get work, then how they get work is *entry*.

The goal of this book is to change how organizations and teams get work so that *work intake* makes more sense. We ended up using the word *intake* because that's what we aspire to see in the organizations we work with. But every time we see bad stuff happen, we can't help but think of it as *work entry*.

1

WHAT IS WORK INTAKE?

Learning Objectives—by the end of this chapter, you will be able to:
> Define work intake
> Give a simple example of a work intake process
> Differentiate between *work entry* and *work intake*

Every entity has a process to decide what to do, how to spend its resources, and how to deploy people—even if that process is to drop everything any time someone asks. Those processes are considered *work intake*. Work intake is not the sexiest topic. There's an old cartoon that depicts a manager standing in front of a room of coders. The manager states, "You keep coding, I'll go get some requirements." This shows how disrespected work intake is as a process. Unless a team has mature (or maturing) processes for working, it is generally not understood. In several recent conversations, we asked individuals and teams how they get the work they were assigned to do. "We triage the work with our product owner," was one end of the spectrum. "The phone rings and somebody's manager tells me what to do," was the other end. We were also accused of being killjoys for bringing up the topic during happy hour.

Most people simply come to work to deliver, so discovering how work enters an organization or team is almost always a touchy subject. Talking about work intake feels like overhead because it happens before you can do the *real* work. When asked about work intake, we are generally given a PowerPoint presentation or a process document to read. Regardless of the processes that are diagrammed, they are never right. Work intake mimics a water leak in a building; it is almost as if it were alive—or had a mind of its own. Work seeks a way to get started. Sometimes it even gets all the way to done. It can enter through the *front door*—tied to strategic plans in the enterprise portfolio. It can also find a *back door* to a team or individual and get done *off the books* (read: unsanctioned). Every level of an organization has a work intake process. This process cascades work to lower levels and informs the levels above it. The problem is that every level also has secret paths to someone who will choose to accept the work. Every one of these paths defines work intake. Every last piece of *started* work has a permanent impact on the trajectory of a firm, product, and team.

A SIMPLE EXAMPLE OF WORK INTAKE IN SCRUM

Scrum is "a lightweight framework that helps people, teams and organizations generate value through adaptive solutions for complex problems."[1] In Scrum, work intake follows a simple flow of steps:

1. People write stories, ideas, or requirements of varying quality
2. Items get evaluated and cleaned up
3. Updated, well-formed stories get added to the backlog, becoming product backlog items (PBIs)
4. Once on the backlog, PBIs get prioritized (and reprioritized)
5. In time, PBIs get pulled into a sprint

In Scrum, the product owner owns the backlog and the prioritization process. They work with the team to determine when to do each item. If real life was this cut and dried, there would be no reason for this book.

---

[1] "The Scrum Guide." Scrum.org, 8/25/2023, https://scrumguides.org/scrum-guide.html.

WORK INTAKE AND AGILE

You won't find the phrase *work intake* in most (if any) agile texts, but that doesn't mean the concept isn't important. Where does all the work that the teams are doing come from? Where exactly does the work that the product owner prioritizes come from? Work is the one common ingredient that every process requires. Whether you're a startup with one Scrum team, or a thousand-person development shop using the Scaled Agile Framework (SAFe®), work has to come from somewhere—otherwise, you wouldn't have a job.

This book will discuss work intake through the lens of the *Agile Manifesto*. Without disciplined work intake, being agile will always be out of reach.

Agile Manifesto Values

Let's take a look at how the value statements from the *Agile Manifesto* pertain to the topic of work intake:

- **Individuals and interactions over processes and tools:** All companies, organizations, and teams have a process they follow when work appears. This can range from ad hoc to well-controlled. There are times when following a structured process could lead to detrimental outcomes for you and your customers. This is where *individuals and interactions* come into play. Mastering work intake requires communication with individuals up and down the value stream.
- **Working software over comprehensive documentation:** This value statement focuses on the outcomes of work intake conversations and processes. If all you do with new work is have conversations and then generate documentation, you're doing it wrong. Customers buy products that work. They won't buy a document that describes how a product should work.
- **Customer collaboration over contract negotiation:** Some of the work that enters your system will come from internal or external customers. Work requests demand conversation and collaboration to ensure transparency and alignment.

- **Responding to change over following a plan:** This value statement screams *relentless prioritization.*

Agile Manifesto Principles

Academics describe empirical approaches using the phrases "fact-based" and "experience-based." Agilists use the phrase "inspect and adapt." They observe, gather facts, and then adapt. Empirical approaches are at the heart of agile because they generate transparency. Let's take a look at how the principles tie to the work intake cycle.

Before Work Enters (Work Intake Enablers)

We call this group of principles *work intake enablers* because they enable people and organizations to master work intake (see Figure 1.1). They shape behavior before work enters an organization or team.

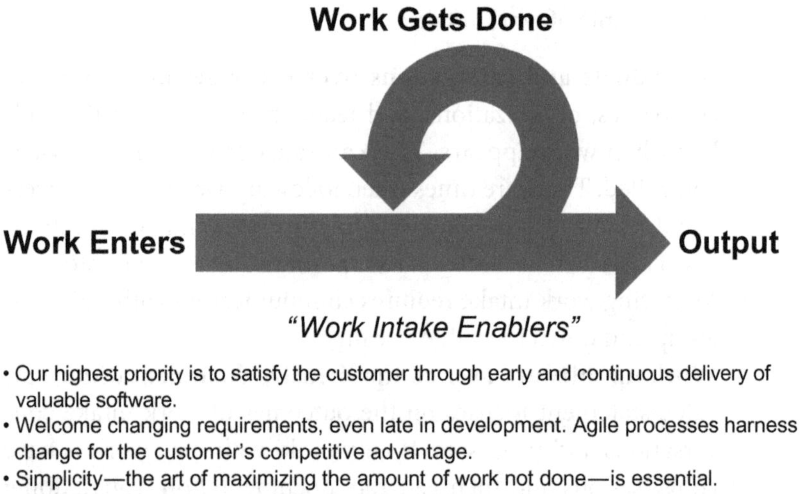

Work Gets Done

Work Enters   **Output**

"Work Intake Enablers"

- Our highest priority is to satisfy the customer through early and continuous delivery of valuable software.
- Welcome changing requirements, even late in development. Agile processes harness change for the customer's competitive advantage.
- Simplicity—the art of maximizing the amount of work not done—is essential.

Figure 1.1   *Agile Manifesto* principles enable work intake.

- **Our highest priority is to satisfy the customer through early and continuous delivery of valuable software:** Every company serves customers. This means that you do the work they ask you to do. It also means that you adjust your priorities because of their priorities.

- **Welcome changing requirements, even late in development; agile processes harness change for the customer's competitive advantage:** *Changing requirements* means a change to the requested work. Those changes count as work intake. This includes new, modified, or canceled backlog items.
- **Simplicity—the art of maximizing the amount of work not done—is essential:** Mastering work intake allows you to do important things. It also enables you to defer things that aren't important.

While Work Is in Progress (Don't Forget These)

We call this group of principles *don't forget these* because they help guide people and teams while work is being done (see Figure 1.2). They also shape behavior while work is being done.

Work Gets Done

Work Enters   **Output**

"Don't Forget These"

- Business people and developers must work together daily throughout the project.
- Build projects around motivated individuals. Give them the environment and support they need, and trust them to get the job done.
- The most efficient and effective method of conveying information to and within a development team is face-to-face conversation.
- Agile processes promote sustainable development. The sponsors, developers, and users should be able to maintain a constant pace indefinitely.
- Continuous attention to technical excellence and good design enhances agility.
- The best architectures, requirements, and designs emerge from self-organizing teams.

Figure 1.2 *Agile Manifesto* principles to keep in mind while doing work.

- **Business people and developers must work together daily throughout the project:** This principle encourages a better understanding of what to build—and why. Diverge from this principle and your work intake process risks misalignment.
- **Build projects around motivated individuals, give them the environment and support they need, and trust them to get the job done:** A *project* is synonymous with the current work. People do the work that enters your system. Mastering work intake ensures that your people are working on high-value items. Doing high-value work is a motivator for lots of individuals.
- **The most efficient and effective method of conveying information to and within a development team is a face-to-face conversation:** When things change—and they always do—these types of interactions are imperative.
- **Agile processes promote sustainable development; the sponsors, developers, and users should be able to maintain a constant pace indefinitely:** Mastering work intake ensures that people aren't overwhelmed by too much work.
- **Continuous attention to technical excellence and good design enhances agility:** This principle is a reminder to leave space for people and teams to do this type of work. While satisfying customer and business needs is imperative, this work is not optional. Failure to leave space for this type of work can slow down future work. It can also disrupt the flow of value coming from your organization.
- **The best architectures, requirements, and designs emerge from self-organizing teams:** Not all work will enter your system with well-understood requests. At times, some special instruction will need to occur. Asking a select group of senior people to do this work creates bottlenecks in your system. This principle acknowledges a need to push this work down to the people and teams on the front lines.

When Work Is Done (Work Intake Outcomes)

We call this group of principles *work intake outcomes* because they result from mastering work intake (see Figure 1.3).

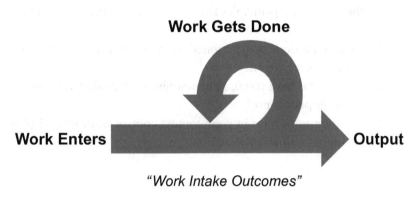

"Work Intake Outcomes"

• Deliver working software frequently, from a couple of weeks to a couple of months, with a preference to the shorter timescale.
• Working software is the primary measure of progress.
• At regular intervals, the team reflects on how to become more effective, then tunes and adjusts its behavior accordingly.

Figure 1.3   *Agile Manifesto* principles are outcomes of mastering work intake.

- **Deliver working software frequently, from a couple of weeks to a couple of months, with a preference to the shorter timescale:** Focus less on trying to grasp what customers want; focus more time delivering what they actually need.
- **Working software is the primary measure of progress:** If you're doing small pieces of work and there's flow in your system, a likely result is working software.
- **At regular intervals, the team reflects on becoming more effective, then tunes and adjusts its behavior accordingly:** Retrospect on the work and adjust. In other words, wash, rinse, repeat.

END-OF-CHAPTER QUESTIONS

Use the following to start a conversation about this chapter's contents:

1. Review your work intake practices. Where is there friction with the values and principles from the *Agile Manifesto*? Where are there gaps?
2. How often does unsanctioned work happen in your context? How does it happen?
3. What terms have you used to describe work intake? What terms do other people use?
4. What types of roles in your context control work intake? (For example, product owners.)

2

WHAT DOES GOOD WORK
INTAKE LOOK LIKE?

> **Learning Objectives**—by the end of this chapter, you will be able to:
> - Understand that there is no single perfect way to control work intake
> - Recognize the nine core principles of work intake
> - Learn how to assess work intake based on the nine core work intake principles

INTRODUCTION

There is no perfect approach to bringing work into an organization or team. Since it involves people, perfection may not be something that can exist in the real world. Good work intake is independent of the framework you follow. How you achieve *good* is dependent on your context.

Some examples of good approaches include:

- Lean portfolio management in the Scaled Agile Framework (SAFe®)

- Program increment planning in (SAFe®)
- Sprint planning (Scrum and large-scale Scrum)
- Queue replenishment (kanban)

Every organization and team leverages its own version of frameworks and business practices. Implementation is a set of trade-offs that define a continuum. Value delivery and sustainable pace sit on either end of this continuum. We make trade-offs between these as work enters. As we do so, we assess whether our work intake approaches are good.

Different contexts demand never-ending trade-offs between maximizing value delivery and a sustainable pace. For example, teams will always choose to balance value delivery and sustainable pace. This is often called achieving a *work-life balance*. Teams do this when they are not under a death march's pressure and control work intake. The trade-offs change when confronted with a production or business emergency. In these cases, teams will sacrifice a sustainable pace to deliver value.

This brings us to the ultimate value delivery/sustainable pace *antipattern*. (An antipattern is a practice that appears to be useful, but in reality, it's ineffective, counterproductive, or leads to unintended negative consequences.) It's the one where everything is an emergency and teams are on a continuous death march. Unfortunately, this antipattern is not an uncommon approach to management. Teams make choices about what value means in order to protect a modicum of sustainable pace. They make these choices to save themselves from burnout. A phrase like *tech debt* obfuscates what's happening. Corners get cut for the sake of making an unsustainable pace more sustainable.

NINE CORE PRINCIPLES

It doesn't matter whether you are using Scrum, kanban, or waterfall. Good work intake requires nine core principles to be present in some form. Evan Leybourn, founder of the Business Agility Institute, calls this type of list a *Don't Forget Model*. For work intake to be good, a team or organization has to do something to cover these principles. Forgoing any of these principles will set you on the path to the proverbial *ninth circle of (work intake) hell*.

The nine core principles for good work intake are:

1. **Prioritization:** Prioritization must occur in a systematic way for all work. Approaches without solid prioritization devolve into randomness during times of stress.

2. **Control:** Work needs to follow a defined path to enter an organization or team. Everyone involved in work intake must have a modicum of discipline and self-restraint. They must also have the wherewithal to hold each other accountable.

3. **Transparency:** All interested parties can see the backlog of work. They also understand the process for maintaining the backlog. When transparency fails, people create conspiracy theories and cheat.

4. **Consistency:** Policies and processes must govern how work gets to the backlog. They must be consistent in their application. Carving policies in stone rarely makes sense. The work intake process should evolve based on context, rather than haphazard change.

5. **Frequency:** The processes governing work intake need to happen on a regular basis. The more dynamic the environment, the more often they should occur.

6. **Preparation:** Work intake is a decision or set of decisions. The work has to be ready before those involved can make a decision. Indecision or ad hoc decisions will yield random outcomes.

7. **Respect:** Respect for the process and participants is critical. Respect is not blind belief.

8. **Consequences:** There must be consequences for violating work intake processes. Jumping the queue is not a victimless crime; everyone else gets to pay the price.

9. **Ownership:** Someone is responsible and accountable for work intake. Without it, the flow of work will emulate water and seek the ground in any way possible.

Think of each of these nine principles as a light dimmer. You can adjust them based on the business context. For example, market changes might dictate that priorities get more frequent examination.

Good work intake is independent of how an organization or team manages work. We've seen agile and plan-based organizations practice disciplined work intake. We've also seen agile organizations that were out of control. The out-of-control organizations did not fare well with these nine principles.

Each of these nine principles reflects a range of behaviors. Two human reaction ranges can still cause trouble:

- **Making monolithic decisions on how the organization and all teams approach the principles:** This is akin to mandating that every team will use Scrum and have a two-week sprint starting on a Tuesday. Unless you are in a very small organization, each team will have a very different set of needs. One size may fit one team some of the time, but not every team every time.
- **The propensity to turn any of these principles to zero:** For example, not requiring preparation for planning or refinement sessions will generate frustration, storytelling, and jumping the queue.

To determine how well a team or organization is handling work intake, assess how people act. Before you do anything else, go and observe the people doing the work. Actions are the outward manifestation of the real culture of a team or organization. The rest is aspiration.

An Example—Sprint Planning in Scrum

The example of sprint planning in this section is not an endorsement of Scrum. We often use Scrum—and it is well understood—but many different approaches are useful. Your context will dictate which approach will work in each situation.

Here is an example of the nine core principles as shown via the sprint planning event from Scrum:

1. **Prioritization:** ✔ The product owner prioritizes the backlog.

2. **Control:** ✔ Work enters a Scrum team via the product backlog and sprint planning.
3. **Transparency:** ✔ Both the product and sprint backlogs are visible to the team and stakeholders.
4. **Consistency:** ✓ Events in Scrum are consistent. Scrum is mute on how to regulate work intake.
5. **Frequency:** ✔ The sprint planning event occurs on a cadence.
6. **Preparation:** ✓ Refinement prepares the product backlog for sprint planning. Backlog refinement is the responsibility of the team and is not a specific event. Conducting refinement events is not a universal convention, but is common.
7. **Respect:** ✓ The Scrum value of respect focuses on the people. Scrum is mute on respect for the process.
8. **Consequences:** ✕ Scrum is mute on this subject. The assumption is that work that doesn't go through sprint planning doesn't get done.
9. **Ownership:** ✔ The product owner manages the backlog and accepts work, therefore, the role has ownership.

(✔ = Fully addressed, ✓ = Partially addressed, ✕ = Not addressed)

Scrum fully addresses five of the nine principles. It somewhat addresses three others and misses on one. Communal convention and peer enforcement will plug the gaps. Collectively, they will keep the process moving in the right direction. This can only happen if teams are aware of the core principles and the reasons to address them.

END-OF-CHAPTER QUESTIONS

Use the following topics to start a conversation about the contents of this chapter:

1. Consider how work gets to your team(s). How does the process address the nine core principles?
2. If you found gaps between practice and principles, what is an experiment that will address one of the gaps? What needs to be in place to run this experiment?

3

WORK INTAKE BASICS

Learning Objectives—by the end of this chapter, you will be able to:

> ‣ Describe the difference between pushing work and pulling work
> ‣ Describe a story-driven context and an interrupt-driven context
> ‣ Define the utilization maximization fallacy
> ‣ Give a general example of flow
> ‣ Describe the happy path

A simple definition of work intake is full of implicit and explicit assumptions. They're based on the type of work, team, and organizations involved. Understanding work intake requires grasping these five concepts:

1. Push versus pull
2. Story-driven versus interrupt-driven
3. Utilization maximization fallacy
4. Flow
5. The happy path

PULL VERSUS PUSH

Pull and *push* are simple four-letter words that are not always understood. A simple definition of *pull* is that teams accept new work when they have the capacity to do it. That work has a reasonable chance of progressing to *done* without interruption. The people doing the work will pull based on the capacity of the system. A Scrum team member says, "I ask the product owner what's next on the backlog when we have the capacity to do more." This is indicative of a work intake process that is built around *pulling* work.

Push, obviously, is the opposite of *pull*. People and teams get work based on the arrival of the work requests. *Push* focuses on demand rather than capacity or flow considerations. The proverbial *squeaky wheel* is a common push approach. Those who yell the loudest get their work started when they want.

Here's an example of a push scenario. A few years ago, we observed a consulting firm that used a push process between sales and delivery. The salespeople sold the work and then pushed the sold work into delivery. There was usually a promised start and end date. The delivery teams scrambled and were often unable to meet the promised dates. There were no winners in this scenario. Sales and delivery did not trust one another. Lack of delivery quality led to unsatisfied customers.

STORY-DRIVEN VERSUS INTERRUPT-DRIVEN

Story-driven and *interrupt-driven* teams have different approaches for managing their work queues. In story-driven teams, work appears as part of a prioritized backlog. Requirements, while they may be dynamic, reflect market or business needs. They're staged, refined, and then *taken* by the team. Scrum is a common mode of operation for story-driven teams.

In interrupt-driven teams, work appears in an unpredictable fashion. Operational support teams are often interrupt-driven. Kanban is a common mode of operation for interrupt-driven teams.

Not every team is story-driven or interrupt-driven. Many teams mix both types of work. One example of this is teams in an IT department. Teams that mix work generally reflect the behaviors of interrupt-driven teams. For example, we worked with a large Scrum team supporting an enterprise resource planning package. But, this team was mixing story-driven and interrupt-driven work. They took on all types of work that appeared—and started it. Because of this, the team was unable to meet their story-driven work commitments. The team would plan a sprint full of stories (story-driven work). Tickets from incidents and important enhancements (interrupt-driven work) would often disrupt the plan. In order to resolve this problem, the team was split into two component teams. One team did story-driven work using Scrum. The second team adopted a kanban(ish) form of Scrum that is often referred to as *Scrumban*.

UTILIZATION MAXIMIZATION FALLACY

All systems—human and/or mechanical—have a capacity. Many organizations mandate teams and leaders to plan for maximizing capacity utilization. They do this by scheduling people (often unfortunately called *resources*) at 100 percent capacity. This approach pushes work to each step in the process. It disregards constraints and bottlenecks. The end result is lots of work started but less work completed. The focus on planning to 100 percent utilization in software teams is counterproductive. Teams that make a habit of running at 100 percent utilization generate waste. Waste includes work sitting around, as well as defects. People also burn out much faster. We call this conundrum the *utilization maximization fallacy*.

You Asked . . .

What is Parkinson's Law? Parkinson's Law states that work expands to fill the time available. Cyril Northcote Parkinson observed that bureaucracies expand over time. "It is a commonplace observation that work expands so as to fill the time available for its completion." Popular management theory has extended the statement to cover all forms of work. If work expands to fill available time, managers should then overload backlogs. This ensures that people spend time in the most efficient manner.

In IT, managers and project managers strive to ensure that 100 percent utilization gets planned and monitored. This is counterproductive because it generates planning errors and compression.

FLOW

Flow is the amount of business value that travels through a process in a specific time. Flow is often measured as a function of pace and consistency. Predictability depends on how work enters, how it's triaged, and constraint exploitation.

Here is a metaphor for flow predictability. Imagine cars moving through a roundabout. Now imagine how cars move through an intersection with stop signs on each corner. Flow in product development should resemble the roundabout. Starting and stopping should be minimal. Flow maximizes the delivery of value by reducing the delay. We will examine flow in greater detail in Section Three.

THE HAPPY PATH

The long evangelized *happy path*—both in waterfall and agile—goes something like this:

1. An enterprise-sized piece of work gets identified by leaders of the organization.

2. That piece of work is then broken into smaller pieces and doled out to different parts of the organization. (A department or division, for example.)

3. The middle level prioritizes the work and decomposes it into even smaller pieces. Teams complete the work in a timely fashion.

Everything flows down the hierarchy to teams that make the magic happen and the enterprise reaps value. While this is an idealized version, it does happen in reality. Although, it doesn't seem to be as repeatable or ubiquitous a pattern as companies expect.

Experiment

Problem: Employees fail to realize that work follows more than one path to get done.

Hypothesis: It behooves everyone to understand how much work follows the happy path and how much does not. The knowledge provides a baseline understanding of where the organization is currently. Only with this understanding can it drive improvement.

Do You Have This Problem?—Questions to Diagnose.

- Can the average employee name any of the company's strategic initiatives?
- Does the work in progress correlate to any of the company's strategic initiatives?
- How often do people do work that isn't tied to any of the company's strategic initiatives?

Experiment: Think about the work your company does and then answer the following questions:

- What percentage of work do you think follows the happy path?
- What percentage of work do your peers or team think follows the happy path?
- What's the difference between both percentages?

The answers to these questions will shine a light on any gaps in assumptions that exist. If the gap is wide, there are likely actions to take to yield a common understanding of how work gets done.

continued

Validation: Confirm the percentage of work that follows the happy path to validate the previous responses.

Example: A product manager surveys a few coworkers to understand how they think work gets down to teams. Half the people think it's based on the company's big initiatives. The other half thinks it's random customer requests. The product manager reviews the backlog to determine where the work that the teams do comes from. The product manager finds that about 75 percent of the work comes from customers. Approximately 25 percent comes from the company's big initiatives. The product manager begins working with the teams to swing this balance to become 50/50.

END-OF-CHAPTER QUESTIONS

Use the following to start a conversation about the contents of this chapter:

1. When have you seen work pushed on a team? When have you seen teams pull work? Which is more common in your context?
2. Do more teams in your context operate as story-driven or interrupt-driven? Why?
3. When teams plan work, do they plan for 100 percent utilization? Why or why not?
4. Can you describe the flow of work in your context?
5. How much work follows the happy path in your organization? How much should it be?

4

WHO CARES ABOUT
WORK INTAKE?

Learning Objectives—by the end of this chapter, you will be able to:
- › Understand an executive's perspective on work intake
- › Understand a customer's perspective on work intake
- › Understand an internal stakeholder's perspective on work intake

Every person makes decisions about what work they do. Some decisions have little or no impact on the direction of the team and organization. Other decisions send ripples upstream and downstream. Without due consideration, it is difficult to know how large an impact any decision will have. Because of this, everyone needs to think about the work they do. Examining three typical groups of stakeholders drives the *who cares* point home.

EXECUTIVES

Executives focus on strategies. They make big bets on behalf of the organization. Their decisions cause significant action. Failure to control work intake at the executive level generates confusion. Value streams, departments, and teams struggle with too many strategic mandates. The organization below the executives can also lose control of work intake. This can delay strategic initiatives.

Experiment

Problem: The bigger the organization, the harder it is to align with strategic initiatives. This results in the people who are doing the work losing sight of why they're doing the work in the first place.

Hypothesis: People will be more committed to their work if they understand how it connects to strategic initiatives.

Do You Have This Problem?—Questions to Diagnose.

Ask people at different levels in the organizational chart the following questions:

- What are the organization's strategic initiatives?
- How do these strategic initiatives relate to the work you (or your team) are doing?
- Which strategic initiative does the work you are doing support?

Experiment: During a team meeting, discuss how the work aligns with strategic initiatives. Show an artifact (video, e-mail, etc.) that describes the organization's strategic initiatives. Invite an executive to attend and speak with the people who are doing the work.

Validation: Alignment to strategic initiatives should impact a product's backlog. Backlog changes reflect how much communication of strategic initiatives needs to continue. Another validation of this experiment will be less visible. Observe how much the team talks about the organization's strategic initiatives. Listen to whether they connect it to the work they're doing. If it isn't often, spend more time talking about how the work connects to strategic initiatives.

Example: A team is in the midst of transitioning from one stream of work to the next. During a team meeting, a team member laments that they will be shifting their focus. One team member says, "I don't know why we're moving from this type of work to this other type. We should keep working on the thing we're working on." Another team member pulls up a recent e-mail from the company's chief technology officer. This e-mail describes the strategic initiative that the new work supports. The team spends a few minutes reviewing the e-mail. The team member who expressed confusion confirms that they now understand the rationale.

CUSTOMERS

Customers are a critical source of change requests for external products. Customers have the most intimate knowledge about how they want to use any product. Their requests range from frustrations to areas for growth. Each request gets triaged and prioritized. Prioritization may also include deciding not to make the change. Every single customer request cannot arrive at the top of the queue. If so, teams will exist in an interrupt-driven death spiral. Technical debt and defects occupy the bottom of the priority list. Because of this, the product becomes more brittle and harder to maintain. In the end, delivery of customer requests slows to a trickle.

INTERNAL STAKEHOLDERS

Not all requests to do work come from customers. Support functions have needs that translate to requests. These requests are often integral to selling the product or other strategic work. This gives these types of requests a feeling of urgency and importance. The feelings associated with these requests can cause them to jump the queue. This displaces work that might be even more important but is not perceived as urgent. Controlled work intake recognizes work as it emerges. The work is then prioritized based on need and value, rather than a gut reaction that the sky is falling.

Experiment

Problem: Software teams cannot always communicate with the people who use their product. Organizational layers exist between the teams and the users. This increases the likelihood of implementation errors.

Hypothesis: Internal stakeholders have a huge impact on work intake. This is because they are often the conduit for any customer request. Different internal stakeholders have a more nuanced understanding of customer needs. This perspective is helpful when prioritizing work.

continued

Do You Have This Problem?—Questions to Diagnose.

Build a set of personas for internal stakeholders. Ask them the following questions:

- How often does each stakeholder have contact with customers?
- What type of customers do they communicate with?
- Which products does each stakeholder generate requests for?
- How is each stakeholder incentivized?

Experiment: Host an internal stakeholder get-together. Get internal stakeholders together in an informal setting to talk about the product. First, the product owner or manager shares the high-level product plan. Then, stakeholders share customer feedback and potential enhancement requests. The session will build a bridge between product and internal stakeholders. It will also provide the information needed for interpreting and prioritizing stakeholder requests.

Validation: Every learning impacts the makeup and prioritization of the product's backlog. This includes the knowledge of the stakeholder personae. It also includes stakeholder input on needs and experiences of customers. The amount of backlog changes is proportional to the need for future communication.

Example: A team has delivered a major enhancement that a customer requested. The backlog of future work is small. The team decided to celebrate the delivery by hosting a happy hour. They invited stakeholders from various departments. Sales, Marketing, Technical Support, and Technical Writing were all included. During the event, the stakeholders shared what they're hearing from customers. They even brainstormed some enhancements to the product. The team members took mental notes of what they heard. They regrouped the next morning to debrief and determine which people to follow up with. The outcome was a backlog that's prioritized to mirror the items that came up during the happy hour.

END-OF-CHAPTER QUESTIONS

Use the following to start a conversation about the contents of this chapter:

1. How often do executives talk about new products (i.e., new work)?
2. What is the team or organization's attitude toward customer requests? Why?
3. How is the customer's perspective included in the work you do?
4. Describe a time when an internal stakeholder made a request to a team or organization. How did they make the request? What was the response from the team or organization?

This book has free material available for download from the
Web Added Value™ resource center at *www.jrosspub.com*

5

THREE LEVELS OF
WORK INTAKE

Learning Objectives—by the end of this chapter, you will be able to:
- ➤ Describe work intake at the organization level, as well as the types of roles that are active at that level
- ➤ Describe work intake at the middle level, as well as the types of roles that are active at that level
- ➤ Describe work intake at the team level, as well as the types of roles that are active at that level
- ➤ Describe common team-level work intake patterns

Most organizational models involve some form of hierarchy. Even flat organizational models, such as Holacracy, have groups that establish vision and strategy. We have adopted a simple model to illustrate the impact of work intake on each level of an organization (see Figure 5.1). Our model is that of an inverted pyramid. This model is a simplification. For example, both of us once worked for the same medium-sized software firm. In that firm, the middle level was three to five sublayers, depending on the division.

Figure 5.1   The three levels of work intake.

This model lets us show how every level has a work intake process. It also lets us show how the work accepted by one layer cascades to lower levels, and vice versa. Each level informs the layer above and below it. All layers must plan and manage work intake—each level evaluating capacity. Every decision impacts each level up and down the chain. The appropriate metaphor here is one of rivers and streams. River and stream are often used as synonyms, but they are not the same thing. Many rivers begin as streams. A bunch of small things (streams) can have a huge impact (they form a river). And there's a correlation here to work intake; it is an additive thing. Even small requests to do work add up and impact the wider enterprise.

You Asked . . .

Are there organizational structures that don't follow classic hierarchies? Yes. There are organizations that don't follow classic corporate hierarchies and power structures. Some organizations start with this mentality. Others evolve to address different cultures and business contexts. Organizational structure impacts the flow of work in an organization. Here are two examples:

continued

- Zappos, an American shoe and clothing retailer, transitioned to using a governance structure called Holacracy. Holacracy distributes the power to make decisions among self-organizing groups. Each group is a *holon*. Each holon operates within a sphere of control based on a charter. Work flows between holons based on members interacting. Think of Holacracy as an operating system. Each holon is an independent service that is executed as needed. For more information, check out *Holacracy: The New Management System for a Rapidly Changing World* by Brian J. Robertson.

- Patagonia, an American retailer of outdoor recreation clothing, is an example of a company that Frederic LaLoux calls *teal*. Teal organizations are flat—forming and reforming to pursue their purpose. Teal organizations embody three key ideas: self-management, wholeness, and evolutionary purpose. For more information, check out *Reinventing Organizations: A Guide to Creating Organizations Inspired by the Next Stage in Human Consciousness* by Frederic LaLoux.

ORGANIZATION-LEVEL WORK INTAKE

Active Roles at This Level

The following roles are often active at this level:

- Portfolio epic sponsor
- Portfolio manager
- Executive (C-level, VP-level)
- (Enterprise or portfolio) agile coach
- Product manager
- Project/program manager
- Director/senior manager
- Customer-facing internal stakeholder
- Customer

How Work Intake Works

Executives and outside forces (e.g., regulation) influence organization-level work intake. Work at this level includes:

- Requests from high-profile customers
- Creation of new products (new value streams)
- Major enhancements to existing products
- Major regulatory changes

Organization-level work represents big bets made on behalf of the company. Work that enters at this level has broad impacts on people, teams, and finances. It is visible to everyone up and down the organizational chart—from executives to regular employees. If you're a public company, this work might even be visible to shareholders and analysts. Communication is critical to ensure alignment. Some common tools include presentations and progress reports at all-hands meetings and quarterly updates. In modern organizations, big, visible charts and dashboards reveal information to the firm. Performance of organizational initiatives impacts annual merit and bonus programs. Success can mean a promotion; failure can mean the end of a career.

MIDDLE-LEVEL WORK INTAKE

Active Roles at This Level

The following roles are often active at this level:

- Agile coach
- Product manager
- Project manager/program manager
- Manager/team lead
- Director/senior manager
- Customer-facing internal stakeholder
- Customer

How Work Intake Works

Executives at the organizational level influence work intake in the middle. In many organizations, vision and high-level objectives get decomposed into smaller pieces. This work flows into divisions, departments, and value chains. If this flow was always hierarchical, it would be easy to understand and track. There are other inputs to be mindful of at this level, though.

Work that enters the middle is not always tied to a big, important, visible, strategic thing. Sometimes, it's an enhancement to a product for a set of customers. Other times, it might be a lean startup-style R&D effort to win new business. Since different types of work enter in the middle, the degree of difficulty to master work intake is high. We'll explore work intake in the middle even further in Section Four of this book.

Bonuses in the middle often include performance on new strategic work, as well as *keep-the-lights-on* work. These types of work, unfortunately, compete with one another for attention. Work enters the middle from many places. It is critical to understand that there is nothing prima facie wrong with that. Things go wrong when there is a lack of transparency.

For more on work intake in the middle, see Chapter 23.

TEAM-LEVEL WORK INTAKE

Active Roles at This Level

The following roles are often active at this level:

- Scrum Master
- Product owner/product manager
- Team member
- Manager/team lead
- Customer-facing internal stakeholder
- Customer

How Work Intake Works

Product development is a team sport. Teams translate needs, requirements, and raw materials into useful goods. Understanding how strategic plans translate into day-to-day activities is not an esoteric activity.

All teams must have a process for gathering and accepting work. Each team's work intake process defines:

- How work gets to teams
- When work gets to teams
- The priority of the work
- Guidance on when to do the work

A controlled work intake process positions a team to meet the organization's needs. It also highlights when strategic and tactical needs are in conflict.

A team's work intake process is the first step in how value flows. After work enters, it is planned, built, and delivered. Because it comes first, the work intake step must not be messed up.

Five Common Team-Level Work Intake Patterns

There are five common patterns of behavior for bringing work into a team. The first is the *gold standard* and the rest are a series of compromises. We will return to the patterns as we explore the causes and solutions of work intake problems.

Prioritized Single Point of Entry (Gold Standard)

In this pattern (see Figure 5.2), a team's work funnels through a single person (usually with support and advice). This person prioritizes the work based on a set of criteria. In Scrum, this is the process a product owner follows to manage a backlog. The team pulls the work from the backlog as capacity is available. The team completes work with minimal delays. This is the gold standard for work intake at the team level.

- **Delivery pattern:** Priority order (close to *first in, first out*)
- **Ability to deliver:** Predictable

Important attributes of this pattern:

1. Work gets prioritized and reprioritized.
2. Work gets broken down to separate the high-priority work from the low-priority.

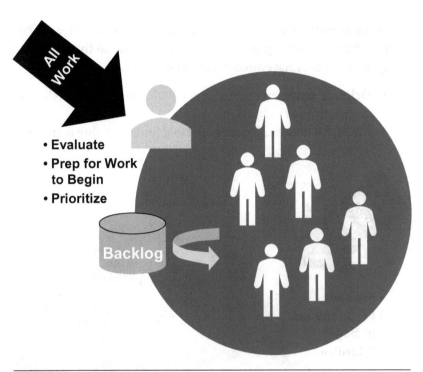

Figure 5.2 The gold standard of work intake.

3. The team weighs in on prioritization and sequencing.
4. The team pulls work to their capacity.
5. *Definition of ready* and *definition of done* exist and get used.

Prioritized Pull with Prioritized Incident Push (Silver Standard)

Tom spent portions of his career with pagers or an on-call cell phone strapped to his belt. To this day, his blood gets pumping when he hears about a juicy production incident. For any organization, making money or delivering a service trumps every other priority. This pattern reflects the reality of teams that work on products/projects. They have to support the production environment at the same time. This work intake pattern is sometimes the best that teams living this reality can do. When something important breaks in production, the team must address the issue (see Figure 5.3). They must attend to this while still doing the work they have already pulled and planned.

- **Delivery pattern:** Priority order with interruptions (close to *first in, first out*)
- **Ability to deliver:** Often predictable (unless quality is an issue)

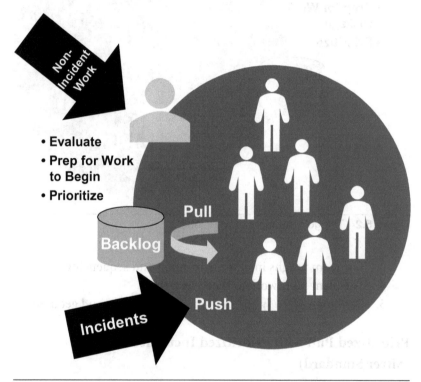

Figure 5.3   The silver standard of work intake.

Front-Door Pull, Back-Door Push

The most important feature of work intake in this pattern is the back door for work to get on the team's plate. In this pattern, work goes from a stakeholder to the team. In some cases, work goes to a specific team member (see Figure 5.4). Sometimes, work gets done *off the books* and interrupts work being pulled by the team. Things like sprint goals and team goals generate conflict, even if work gets done under the radar. This makes for a lethal cocktail. The efficacy and predictability of the team gets compromised.

- **Delivery pattern:** Semi-erratic
- **Ability to deliver:** Unpredictable, but not too terrible

One reason this pattern exists is that everyone can see the prioritization process. This visibility makes it feel like things are under control. The reality is that they are not. This scenario resembles an infestation of carpenter ants. The damage occurs long before the problem is obvious.

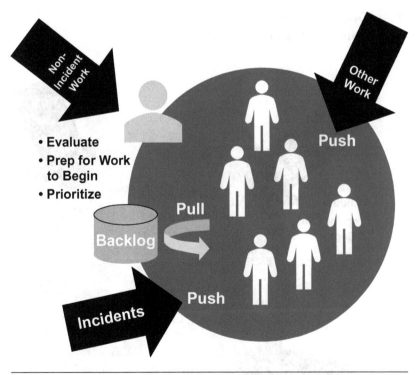

Figure 5.4 Work gets pulled and pushed.

Prioritized and Unprioritized Push with Incident Flow

The final in-between case is one notch better than a free-for-all. At least some of the work has a priority and is visible (see Figure 5.5). The combination of push and back-door intake of work generates a mess. Frequent outcomes include poor employee morale, poor product quality, and irritated stakeholders. People in this pattern rationalize it by using phrases like:

- "We must be responsive."
- "Saying *no* is not an option."
- "This is a dynamic and exciting environment."

This scenario never ends well.

- **Delivery pattern:** Erratic
- **Ability to deliver:** Unpredictable

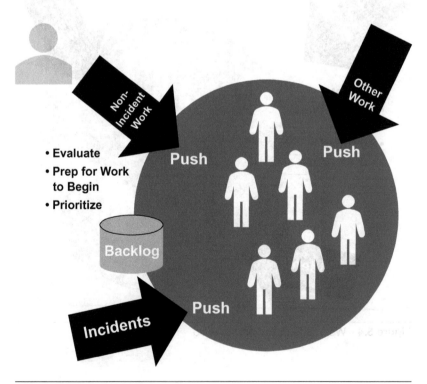

Figure 5.5 Slightly better than nothing.

This approach is always a reflection of deeper issues in the organization.

Free-for-All

In this pattern, each person on the team sees themselves as a free agent. They are out to maximize the perception of their individual utility, so they accept work as they see fit (see Figure 5.6). Work is either pushed to individuals, or individuals pull work without permission. This is the worst-case scenario for work intake.

- **Delivery pattern:** Unpredictable
- **Ability to deliver:** Inconsistent

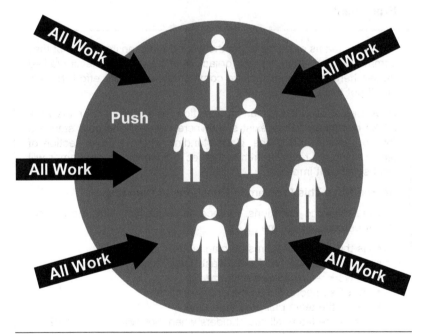

Figure 5.6   Work intake as free agency.

Conclusion

Teams find themselves operating in one of these five patterns for a reason. Many times, those reasons are not of their own making. Rather, they are accommodations to behaviors the organization chooses not to address. Teams don't own pay policies within organizations. Being able to recognize where a team lies on the work intake continuum is a step toward improvement. Ideas and coaching techniques can help move the team from chaos to predictability.

Teams are the day-to-day implementation of work intake; good or bad. When work intake is haphazard, significant time and effort gets lost to churn—churn is meaningless work. People who are not engaged in meaningful and impactful work seek employment elsewhere. Failure to control work intake not only impacts efficiency and efficacy. It kills engagement and motivation.

Experiment

Problem: Teams often fail to get the work done in an iteration that they commit to completing. It's not for lack of effort—they've never worked harder. Iteration reviews include comments like, "Great effort, but we didn't get there."

Hypothesis: Each team in an organization lies somewhere on the work intake continuum. They exist somewhere between the gold standard for work intake and chaos. Understanding where a cross-section of teams stand will reveal common themes. Influencing these themes will yield significant impacts.

Do You Have This Problem?—Questions to Diagnose.

Ask the following questions. Preface each question with the phrase, "What percent of the time . . ."

- Is the work that teams do plannable?
- Can teams say "no," or at least "later," when reasonable?
- Is work reviewed and prioritized?
- Does someone act as the priority police?
- Does the team pull prioritized work?
- Does the team tell stakeholders when they will deliver work?
- Is work completed without spending time on hold?

Plug the answers you received into the following key:

- Good   100–81%
- Neutral   80–60%
- Problematic   59% or less

continued

Experiment: In a retrospective (or similar working session), ask each of the previous questions. Use a planning poker approach with a modified deck. Take three cards—1, 3, 5—five representing good and one representing problematic. The results of each question will identify a core set of behavioral issues.

After discussing each question, identify one or two action items. These are things the team can do that will influence work intake behavioral patterns. Coaches should look for overarching themes requiring organizational interventions to influence.

Validation: Validation must focus on changes in the behavior(s) the experiment is trying to influence. Keep the original answers to each question as a baseline. Then, ask the questions again, after the intervention.

Example: A development team recognized they had lots of *tickets* in progress. The tickets were a mix of enhancements and production defects. They were starting more work than they could ever hope to finish in a sprint. They decided to explore causes during their end-of-sprint retrospective. After establishing context, each member of the team created three sticky notes using the numbers 1, 3, and 5. The facilitator asked the team each of the aforementioned questions, one at a time. Using a planning poker approach, each team member revealed a number. The team reached consensus for each question through discussion and re-voting. The team found that they felt they did not have the ability to say "no" to work. "How can you say *no* to production defects?" asked one of the team members. During the discussion, they recognized they were pulling too much story work. They had a consistent flow of defects to keep them busy. They decided that they did have the ability to say "no" to some types of work—in this case, story work. They agreed to plan less story work during sprint planning. They also realized that more than half of their work was production defects and support. They decided to return to that issue if the work-in-progress problem persisted.

HIERARCHY AND FATALISM: A CAUTION

Fatalism in the workplace is the belief that you can't control or influence the work you do or how you do it. Engagement is a measure of commitment, motivation, and involvement. Engagement impacts a person's work, their colleagues, and their organization. An engaged person is passionate about their work. Hierarchy defines the levels of authority, responsibility, and decision making within an organization. A simpler definition is the *chain of command*. With few exceptions, hierarchy is a fact of life.

Hierarchy, fatalism, and engagement intertwine. The relationship between these concepts is complex. The right kind of hierarchy provides structure and mitigates risk. The same structure can, at a moment's notice, become a boat anchor. Hierarchy must be flexible and adaptable—in essence, agile—to be effective and efficient. Unfortunately, most human institutions lose flexibility once they mature. Jonathan Lee, agile trainer and coach at Vitality Chicago Inc., described how hierarchy can have pros and cons:

> *Hierarchy can be good, providing structure for employees to focus on their roles to become masters of it. From a growth perspective, it may limit their creativity and ability to innovate because the hierarchy is there to maintain that status quo.*

Lee's words highlight the complexity of interacting with real people in real organizations. Anthony Mersino, president of Vitality Chicago Inc., voiced another potential downside of hierarchy:

> *Hierarchy can slow or stop innovation if conversations with peers in related groups are stifled. Things have to go up the chain for approval.*

All organizations have hierarchies—even families. The concept of hierarchy is fine; that is until it passes the point where enough structure becomes too much. The overhead generates plaque in the organization's decision-making arteries. When decisions become hard to make and change, fatalism rears its head.

Determining how much structure is enough but not too much is not a simple algebraic equation. Hierarchy causes a differential of power between those at the top and those at the bottom. *Power distance* is the term for how accepting or tolerant a person (or a group) is of that power differential. While every person is different, several attributes can influence power distance. For example, national or tribal culture can influence power differentials. Clearly Cultural has assessed the power distance for a wide group of countries.[2] The data states that India has a high power distance. This suggests an acceptance of a higher degree of power differential. The United States has a lower power distance. The lower the power distance, the more people tend to challenge authority and power imbalances. Power distance in a team or in a company is not monolithic. Factors that cause variation include leadership style, team composition, and organizational culture.

Organizational culture anchors the belief in hierarchy. Organizations with strong hierarchies hire for belief in the hierarchy. They generate rules and policies that reinforce and defend the hierarchy. In *Starship Troopers*, Robert A. Heinlein described how the Mobile Infantry enforced the chain of command through rules and punishment. While this comes from a fictional novel, the same basic behavior is present in the workplace. Strong hierarchies use fatalism as a tool to repress challenges to authority. Returning to thoughts by Jonathan Lee:

> *It [hierarchy] reduces the ability to be agile and try new and different things as it requires hierarchy buy-in. This is even more challenging when the hierarchy is filled with managers rather than leaders.*

Every change agent must work on reducing power distance and the strength of the hierarchy, or they will fail. Change is not easy; hierarchies will fight back. You will hear phrases like, "That's not the way we do it here." As a change leader, you can fall prey to the narcotic of fatalism.

There are pitfalls to hierarchies. The prevailing attitude in the agile community is that hierarchy has value, but only to a point. A well-understood and compact chain of control is useful. The caveats to the term *useful* include understood and compact. While some hierarchy is good, too much is not. Hierarchies grow until they come to find a tipping point, at which time they become too heavy or too stolid and protective. Past a certain point, they dampen engagement and yield mediocrity without intervention. There are all sorts of good reasons

---

[2] "Power Distance Index." Clearly Cultural, 7/28/2023, clearlycultural.com/geert-hofstede-cultural-dimensions/power-distance-index/.

for organizations to react in this fashion. Mediocrity in a competitive environment is a harbinger of a death spiral.

One of the troubling aspects of hierarchy is the appearance of denied responsibility. Individuals feel they are not responsible for certain actions or decisions because they were following orders or instructions. You won't have to tax your memory to dredge up incidences where you have heard someone say, "I was only doing what I was told." Rigid command-and-control hierarchies provide space for fatalism to emerge. Layers of hierarchy make people feel cut off from participating in decision making. There is little reason for them to feel any responsibility for their actions.

The relationship between hierarchy, engagement, and fatalism is a balancing act. The problem often boils down to empowerment and aligning with a common goal. The combination of delegation and empowerment reduces the potential for blame-shifting and hierarchy-driven fatalism. Aligning to a common goal provides a purpose for people to rally around. Recognize that aligning to a goal is not the same as receiving a goal. Aligning to a common goal is powerful. A strong goal provides fertile ground for a sense of belonging to grow, leading to resilience and engagement. Combining empowerment and goal alignment helps to push back the forces of fatalism.

Knowing the solutions and acting on those solutions are two very different things. It is easy to accept that how we lead and how we work with others is *how it's done*. Fatalism can exist anywhere. When fatalism combines with hierarchy, the only reaction to work entering a system is to say, "Yes," and "When do you want it done?"

END-OF-CHAPTER QUESTIONS

Use the following to start a conversation about the contents of this chapter:

1. Map the inverted pyramid model in this section to your context. Ensure that you identify an organization level, middle level, and team level. Which level do you interact with most? Which level do you interact with least? Why?
2. Review the common team-level work intake patterns. Which ones have you seen recently? What were the circumstances? Can you describe how the patterns impacted the team?

MID-CHAPTER QUESTIONS

6

WORK INTAKE ANTIPATTERNS: WHEN WORK INTAKE GOES WRONG

> **Learning Objectives**—by the end of this chapter, you will be able to:
> - Describe work intake antipatterns
> - Understand how work intake problems ripple into other organizational problems

Work intake is not an esoteric discussion. Real operational and people problems occur when we get it wrong. A very poor work intake process allows anyone to give work to the team at any time. This work gets done based on their own perception of value, urgency, and importance. While this sounds crazy, ad hoc work intake is more common than most leaders know. Teams cannot be efficient and effective when work gets pulled in an uncontrolled way. These same issues occur for any team at any level of the organization. Disciplined programs and teams control work intake. Long-term ad hoc work intake poses enormous risks. A disciplined approach to work intake evaluates and prioritizes work. This ensures that the most important and urgent work gets done before other work.

DISRUPTED WORK

Pushing new work to the team after planning is called an *interruption*. Interruptions disrupt the current flow of work and thought within a team. What happens when you're concentrating on reading and someone asks you to do something else? It's an interruption. Interruptions reduce effectiveness and efficiency because they cause rework. There is no shortage of interruptions in the field of knowledge work. Thinking, creating, considering, and collaborating are all examples. Knowledge workers have to remember where they were as far as diagnosing the problem. They also have to remember how they were planning to solve *the problem*, and what they were going to do next. The longer the interruption, the bigger the impact.

EVERYTHING ELSE IS LATE

Work that enters outside of standard work intake processes stops other items for a period of time. Stopping one piece of work often causes ripple effects. Unless each developer can perform the tasks needed without support or collaboration, this can lead to incomplete key initiatives and rising technical debt. Costs to ship products could increase, while innovation decreases.

REDUCED TRUST

Undisciplined work intake leads to reduced efficiency and late deliveries of committed work. This harms trust between team members, teams, stakeholders, and leadership. Lack of trust causes huge side effects, such as employee turnover.

LEADERSHIP AND TRUST

The ability to control and pull work requires leadership. Teams need leadership so they can self-organize. Leadership also helps teams manage their approach to business problems they are solving. Teams that control how work enters have an outward mindset. Teams with an outward point of view focus on doing the work that delivers the most value.

Along with leadership comes the need for bi-directional trust. The organization must trust that teams will pursue the goals laid out by the product owner. The organization also must trust that teams will deliver. Organizations that promote or allow jumping the queue will never have trust. Trust occurs when actions are transparent and predictable.

When someone outside the team makes choices for the team, control replaces trust. Command and control is a management style used in low trust environments—so is micromanagement. These styles are at odds with the philosophies of knowledge work. They are also at odds with agile and lean.

LACK OF SAFETY

The following factors make it difficult or unsafe to reject work when it's pushed into a team:

- **Dollars and cents:** This refers to the method by which each level of the organization is being incentivized/paid. People will generally do what they think is in their financial best interest. Incentives that favor output over outcomes lead to the tendency to say "yes" to as much work as possible. This causes problems, such as technical debt. Those problems get ignored or spun to be someone else's problem.
- **Failure is punitive:** Leaders insist that teams improve, yet they punish experiments that fail. The freedom to try new ideas is critical for improvement. Punishing failure leads to playing it safe. This reduces innovation and means that teams get more done only by cutting corners.
- **Someone else will do it:** Someone else will always say "yes". We've overheard a team being told by their manager that they weren't being team players. Their crime? They said they would not have the capacity to do a piece of work for a sprint or two. The manager mentioned that the team of contractors down the hall would be glad to tackle the work. The manager then asked why

the organization needed the team that did not have capacity to do the work they were requesting.
- **Power dynamics:** Leaders leverage mismatches of power to get to "yes". Tom followed the manager in the aforementioned example down the hall. He listened to the manager pressure the contractors to accept the work. "I will remember your answer when we renew the contract," was actually uttered to the entire team. In this case, a mismatch of power precluded saying "no".

Work intake is often synonymous with shoving work into a pipeline. Malformed expectations are part of this definition. So are unrealistic ideas of when those expectations will emerge in polished form. For many, the concept of work intake is all about putting pressure on teams and people to do more; often more than they can do without cutting corners. Many team leads and managers struggle with work intake, causing them to ask, "Who is responsible?" A knee-jerk reaction is to ask them to hold up a mirror. Teams always bear at least some responsibility. Ownership of the problem lies with senior leadership. They create and own the culture of the organization. Their words and actions need to match.

Senior leaders must foster an environment that makes controlling work intake safe. Doing so begins by changing leadership incentives. Senior leaders cannot let other leaders off the hook—or even the teams themselves. Everyone up and down the organizational chart needs to understand the implications of saying "yes." Delivery dates come from understanding what's in the pipeline and what teams can deliver. *The Mythical Man-Month*, a book by Frederick P. Brooks, Jr., proved that adding people to a late software project makes it later.[3] Using sprints or iterations hasn't changed Brooks' message. Saying "yes" to everything is a prescription for disaster. Senior leaders: you own it; fix the culture.

---

[3] Brooks, Fred. *The Mythical Man-Month: Essays on Software Engineering*, Addison-Wesley, Boston, MA, 1975.

EVERYTHING IS STARTED, NOTHING IS DONE

Work in progress (WIP) piles up when anyone can bring work to the team with the expectation that it will start immediately. When more work enters a team or value stream than leaves, we have neglected WIP. Picture someone who rarely washes their dishes. At some point, the sink will overflow and all manner of bacteria will form. Neglected WIP begins to decompose. If you are being rewarded for starting work rather than finishing it, you are being paid to neglect WIP.

HERDING

Herding is an example of poor work intake behavior. Herding is a pattern where an individual or team acts based on the behavior of others. It is like the children's game follow-the-leader.

Let's look at a real-world example from a past organization that one of us worked with. In this organization, the perception of being helpful led to bonuses and promotions. The software development group had to install a significant Software-as-a-Service package. The request was to do so before Thanksgiving. The rationale was that doing so would not impact the retail part of the business. But, in reality, the date was absurd. The Chief Information Officer (CIO) gathered teams together to determine if the work was doable. They went around the room asking for input. The answer from each team was "no" until a single team said "yes." In quick succession, everyone changed their minds and played follow-the-leader. The affected teams exhibited herd behavior. As soon as one team broke from the pack, everyone followed. The cascade worsened when the CIO muttered "thank you" after the first two teams said "yes." Herding in decision making took "no" off the table. In the end, the project failed and numerous people (other than the CIO) were asked to find employment elsewhere.

Herding is response-driven; it is often a response to fear and uncertainty. Animals herd as a protection mechanism. Herding makes it more difficult for predators to take advantage of an individual. Herding plays a similar role in decision making. In our example, until one team broke the pattern, everyone had the same answer. The perception was that everyone was being unhelpful. As soon as one team broke rank and another team followed, it became easy to brand the teams that were saying "no" as not being team players. This type of behavior increases risk. Following the leader in this circumstance is rational economic behavior.

Signaled social influence triggers herding. Humans change their behavior to adapt to the environment. Peer pressure and socialization are tools to send signals that establish behavioral boundaries. In our example, the CIO's muttered comment was an explicit signal to the other teams to change course. Perceived helpfulness was an important input into the organization's review process. It generated subconscious guidance for acceptable behavior.

Herding occurs in almost every human enterprise. The behavior is not prima facie good or bad. Yet, playing follow-the-leader can take away the ability to control work intake. The flow of work can bottleneck and slow to a crawl. Teams that can't say "no" when it makes sense will find it difficult to deliver value.

END-OF-CHAPTER QUESTIONS

Use the following to start a conversation about the contents of this chapter:

1. Which of the work intake antipatterns in this chapter have you seen recently? What were the circumstances? What were the outcomes?

2. Are there other work intake antipatterns that you have seen? What were the circumstances? What were the outcomes?

3. Describe a time where a work intake process went wrong. What impact did it have on you? What impact did it have on the team? What impact did it have on the company?

Section One

Conclusion

Teams and organizations *need* to obsess about controlling work intake. There will always be urgent and important items that appear on the horizon to deal with. Unplanned and unsanctioned work should be rare for most development teams and programs.

You Asked . . .

What does a good request to do work look like? We've seen all sorts of requests to do work come to a team. We've seen items in an electronic ticketing system written up like a doctoral thesis. We've also seen literal drawings on napkins. In our experience, a well-formed request to do work includes the following:

- Why the work is important to do (including any relevant customers)
- What the work entails (the outcome)
- Whether the request includes incremental deliveries (i.e., something the customer needs now, something that's up next, or something that may come later)
- How critical it is to do the work (i.e., priority)
- Whether there are any expectations around delivery (i.e., a date)

Requests that enter with this information are unambiguous. There are no assumptions.

Organizations can standardize the request process with a "definition of ready." This can be very useful in promoting consistency across large quantities of people. There is a risk to using artifacts like this, though. There are rich conversations to be had around work intake. Those conversations are much more than going through the motions of a checklist.

Section One

Introspection

A WORK INTAKE CASE STUDY AS A BUSINESS NOVELLA, CHAPTER 1

James (who identifies as they/them) recently left the world of consulting to join Dandelion Software and Services—a Fortune 500 firm—as a full-time employee. During the interview process for a job leading an agile transformation, a few of the interviewers asked how they would coach an organization to get communication flowing between Product Management and Engineering. This was presented as a hypothetical scenario. During their first week on the job, James realized that these questions weren't hypothetical scenarios; Dandelion Software and Services has this very problem.

One of the symptoms James starts hearing about is the existence of two backlogs—one *owned* by Product Management and the other *owned* by Engineering. Neither backlog represents exactly what the executives think is really happening. James begins observing the events of the agile team they will be working with. Their observations suggest that the product owner is much more aligned with Engineering than Product Management. This is causing business-facing features to be prioritized lower than other work. James wonders if the product owner is too close to the technical team. This could also be a reflection of a common organizational problem.

During planning, anything related to a technical issue is acted on immediately without any discussion. As James settles in, they get better visibility into the goals of the organization and what the teams are

supposed to be working on. Every team James talks with is over capacity and working on a wide range of initiatives, rather than the new
product being touted in the marketplace. The company's executives
have forecasted that this new product will generate the lion's share of
revenue growth for the firm over the next several years. Unfortunately,
the new product rollout has been delayed. Nobody seems to be able to
forecast the new delivery date range.

James recognizes that everyone is busy doing the work they believe
is the most valuable. There is evidence that time and effort is spent
building backlogs and prioritizing those backlogs. Just that morning,
James stopped to watch a prioritization exercise being held in a conference room with at least 50 participants (in-person and virtual). The
facilitator pointed out that everyone's input was important. The features for the new product were not at the top of the to-do list; other
work and priorities were seeping into day-to-day activities. As James
excused themselves to find coffee, they thought work intake appears to
be a larger problem than anyone really knows.

As a first step, James decides to get an understanding of where work
enters the organization's flow. James also wants to know how different reality is from the plan. Organizational self-knowledge is the first
step before change can be accomplished. Focusing on the organization
most intimately involved with the new project, James gathers together
a cross-section of managers, team leads, and directors. Once together,
this group uses a simplified inverted pyramid model of the organization to get workshop attendees to answer the following questions:

- Fill out the top three ways that work enters at each of the following levels. Work enters via:
    □ Organization
    □ Middle
    □ Team
- For the organization, middle, and team levels, fill in the following:
    □ "People ASSUME _____% of work enters here."
    □ "In my experience, _____% of work enters here."

- For "Happy Path (this is the executive's view) Decomposition," fill in the following:
  - □ "People ASSUME ____% of work enters here."
  - □ "In my experience, ____% of work enters here."

The goal is less about precision than to identify where perceptions and reality diverge. As heads go down to start to work, Larry from Sales asks, "Happy path? Is that where everyone sings 'Kumbaya'? I don't get it." No one laughs, but James sees other heads nodding in agreement.

James responds, "The happy path is when strategic work gets broken down so that departments and teams turn it into something you can sell. If there's a significant difference between the happy path and a path where everyone provides input, there's a lot of stress in the organization."

The participants complete their own version. Then, James leads the group in completing a consensus view of the responses. The responses show a large amount of work entering at the middle-management level. This means the teams have far less time to spend on strategic initiatives (see Figure S1.1).

The biggest discrepancies between experience and assumptions are at the middle-management level. This breakdown in communication is a big problem. The middle level is the connector between strategic vision and tactical implementation. The middle is no different than a car's transmission. The gear translates the power, so the wheels turn. The transmission fluid absorbs and then dissipates the heat due to friction. Discrepancies kill trust and agility.

In every organization James has worked in, there's been the assumption that middle management accepts new initiatives. Meanwhile, those same middle managers politic for the needs of their teams and favorite products. For one of James's workshop participants, more work enters the flow at the middle level than anyone assumed. Work entering at this level displaces the strategic initiatives identified by the executives. A simple comparison of expectations indicates a mismatch. The executives expect teams to spend 90 percent of their time on strategic

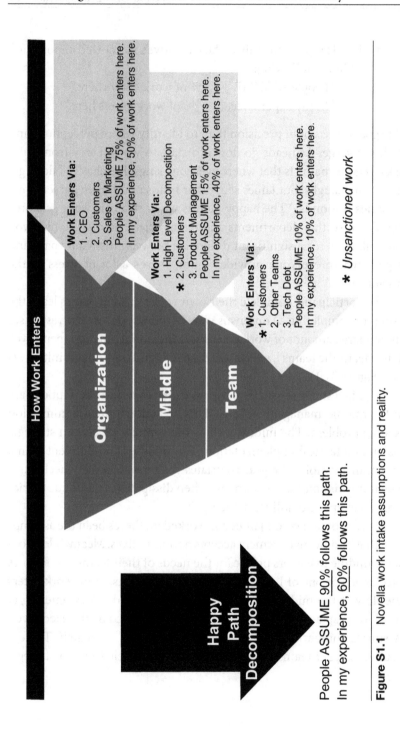

Figure S1.1   Novella work intake assumptions and reality.

initiatives. The reality is that only 50 percent of work is strategic initiatives. James knows there are lots of reasons for this behavior. At this point, it is impossible to identify what is driving the behaviors. James's hypothesis is that everyone is doing the best they can based on the information at hand. Still, change must happen.

EXECUTING NEW IDEAS

It may seem provocative to suggest that you will never be agile if you cannot control work intake. It is not that you can't hold daily Scrums or periodic retrospectives. Rather, you will never derive *all* the value possible from those events. Start your journey by considering how work gets to you or your team.

- **Step 1:** Think long and hard about how work finds a way to get started. Don't assume that work actually follows the patterns it's supposed to follow. How many times have you heard that the product owner prioritizes work for a Scrum team? And then, in the next breath, you listened to a team member accept a new task from another stakeholder? As we have said before, work is like a leak in your roof; you must find where the leak starts before you can patch the problem.
- **Step 2:** Record the three most common ways that work enters each of the following levels:
  - □ Organization
  - □ Middle
  - □ Team

  If you are conducting this activity with a group, define each level of the organization. Groups will generate more than three ways that work enters for each level. Coming to a consensus on the top three for the group is insightful (see Figure S1.2).
- **Step 3:** Next, consider how much work you perceive enters at each level. This is work that does not flow from the layer above. Record your perception. After recording your perception, consider the amount others assume enters at each level. Record

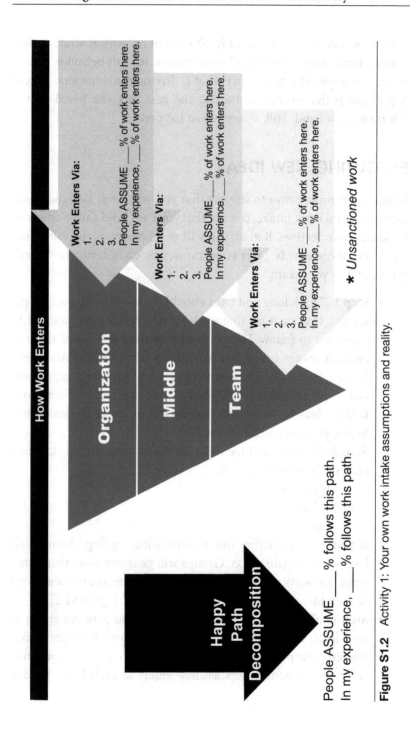

Figure S1.2   Activity 1: Your own work intake assumptions and reality.

those assumptions. How different are your perceptions from the assumptions of others? Why is there a difference?

If you are doing this exercise as a group, have each person record their own personal perceptions. Then, come to a consensus on the assumptions of everyone. How hard was it to generate a consensus?

- **Step 4:** Consider how the organization's leaders think work flows from strategic to tactical. This is the *happy path*. Again, consider both the assumed flow and your perceptions based on your experience.
- **Step 5:** Debrief (group or introspection) using the following questions:
  - **Pyramid percentages**
    - How is your inverted pyramid *weighted*?
    - Does more work enter at the top (organization) than lower levels? Or vice versa?
  - **Assumptions versus experiences**
    - Did these match?
    - Where are the biggest discrepancies? Why?
  - **Happy path**
    - How often does this actually happen in your experience?
    - What's the trigger for this to happen?
    - Does your organization have a way to monitor and report on how work is inputted (and where) in the flow of work?

Section Two

Section Two

Section Two

Work Intake Basics: Prioritization and Sequencing

Section Contents

SECTION INTRODUCTION

Understanding work intake is part of the larger value development and delivery picture. Determining priorities and sequencing work across teams and organizations is another part. Decisions and boundaries are magnets for antipatterns.

"In what order will work get done?" is as old a question as "How long will it take?" This is because the word *order* equates to prioritization and sequencing. We are going to cover both concepts in depth.

Ordering work begins by defining priority, then sequencing. After that, things get complicated. With people involved, patterns can become antipatterns. The time comes for process improvement. Like prioritization, communication and conversation are also key to sequencing.

7

PRIORITIZATION

Learning Objectives—by the end of this chapter, you will be able to:
- ▸ Define the word *priority*
- ▸ Describe why prioritization takes place
- ▸ Describe what a priority is

Identifying what work to do is only part of the work intake equation. Figuring out what is most important (and why) is next. This is true at all levels of the organization.

PRIORITY

Priority is a construct to generate a perception of order. Left to our own devices, each of us uses our own bias to determine what is important. This section includes our ideas on the topic. A key piece of prioritization is ensuring that everyone understands how it's done.

Prioritization done well supports the Agile Manifesto Principle, "Welcome changing requirements, even late in development. Agile processes harness change for the customer's competitive advantage." We want our business or our client to be competitive, if for no other reason than it protects our jobs.

Deciding which piece of work goes first is a vexing question in any organization. Every organization finds a set of tools to help sift through the portfolio of what is possible. Some organizations have central portfolio control. In organizations that don't, each department or team may have its own set of criteria to decide which job to do first. Doing nothing until someone starts yelling is a valid prioritization technique; so is assuming that everything is important. We've not seen those techniques yield successful outcomes for people or companies. We will explore prioritization antipatterns later on. We will also explore techniques for prioritization that we have found successful. These range from *the squeaky wheel technique* to a very detailed cost-benefit analysis.

WHY WE PRIORITIZE

The act of prioritization creates order out of chaos. In today's world, individuals, teams, and even organizations try to do thousands of things at once. The cult of *multitasking* promotes starting everything—then, juggling and time-slicing to appear busy. *Busy* is often confused with *effective*. Smaller, less impactful, work often gets completed before the important work. We're reminded of Stephen Covey's legendary analogy of rocks, pebbles, and sand in a jar. If you fill a jar with sand, there will be no room for the rocks. In the analogy, the sand is less important work. Rocks represent the most important work.

What's most important can—and will—change. This means that prioritization is a point-in-time exercise. In a typical team that works on features and incidents, importance and urgency wax and wane. This leads to the need to reassess priority on a periodic basis. Without an approach for prioritizing work, attention will flow to the wrong thing. It could be to whoever is yelling the loudest or to items that will provide the quickest hit of endorphins. "Prioritization is important because it allows you to give your attention to tasks that are important and urgent so that you can later focus on lower priority tasks."[4]

Left to our own devices, our actions reflect our prioritization process. The Division of Motor Vehicles leverages a *first-in, first-out* approach. Those who have input into how prioritization occurs feel like they're in control. It can have the opposite feeling for those on the outside. When prioritization is a team game, there is less chance of anyone feeling like a victim.

Whether real or perceived, prioritization is a mechanism to highlight what is important. It creates order in a chaotic world. Prioritization that is done well reduces stress and leads to the delivery of more value.

The Role of Risk

Sometimes the most important thing mitigates exposure to risk. In other words, prioritization helps remove risk from your work. For example, an enterprise software company is deploying their software to a client. This is the largest client in the company's history. When the deal hit the newswire, the enterprise software company's stock price moved up (and to the right). During deployment, an issue prevented the client from *going live* with the software. Risk is everywhere in this rudimentary example. The company ran the risk of losing its largest client before it even started using the software if it could not fix the issue in a timely fashion. Even if the client was mollified, there was still financial risk and public relations risk. If news of this failed deployment leaked, other large companies would take note. The company had a literal *all-hands-on-deck* situation. The amount of risk inherent in that scenario meant that they could not ignore it. The issue got prioritized and worked on.

---

[4] Prioritization—Definition and why it's important." Priority Matrix, 7/19/2023, appflu ence.com/productivity/prioritization-what-is-prioritization-and-why-its-important/.

The Role of Quality

Prioritization is a tool to ensure that quality is being built into the product. We've worked in organizations and teams that have different perspectives on quality. Some choose to build quality in from the very beginning (the best approach). They do things like automated testing throughout the product development life cycle. Other firms choose to wait on ensuring quality. They do things like a months-long death march of manual testing before release. In both approaches, the work to ensure quality gets prioritized for that reason, but at different times and with different impacts.

Quality is a word that seems coupled with the phrase *technical debt*. Both terms conjure images of *bug backlogs* and *triage teams*. Neither of those are often viewed as desirable by the people doing the work, but both are essential if your firm has chosen to let quality issues fester.

WHAT IS A PRIORITY?

The simplest definition of the term prioritization is *determining what is most important*. The whole premise of priority is that a group of people have a shared perspective and definition. That perspective may vary, which can be troublesome. For example, an internal stakeholder has a different perspective than actual paying customers. But, in order for a group of people to function, there must be at least a rough consensus about what *prioritization* means. Let's take a look at three different sources that describe how to use and define the word *priority*.

In his book *Monotasking*, Staffan Nöteberg outlines D. W. Houge's 1970 paper,[5] in which Hogue described the following prioritization approaches:

1. **Relative priority:** Work all priorities at the same time, but emphasize the most important. In practice, this is often the case

---

[5] Hogue, W. D. "What does Priority Mean?" in *Business Horizons* 13(6), 1970.

when teams start everything as work presents itself. This leads to *work-in-progress* issues. When everything is a priority, nothing is a priority.

2. **Spillover priority:** Put all effort to the top priority until it's done. Then, when it is done, shift effort to the next priority. This is the type of priority that Nöteberg uses as part of the "Short List" concept in *Monotasking*. This works well with the agile concept of *stop starting and start finishing*.

3. **In-case-of-conflict priority:** Do everything with equal emphasis, unless conflict between projects occurs; then, adjust based on the conflict. This is *the squeaky wheel* approach to prioritization.

4. **Completion priority:** Give priority to things that are easy to finish. This approach was recently described by a colleague as *the low-hanging fruit approach*. People and teams have a list of shorter items that they use to fill gaps between larger items. Priority on the list is not linked to value, but rather to duration. *Weighted shortest job first* is a variant of this approach that adds value weighting.

Hogue's perspective shows that there is a wide range of ways to use and define priority. The fact that different people use different frameworks to define priority is not a shock.

Another approach to defining and assessing priority is the classic Eisenhower Matrix (see Figure 7.1). It is named after the former United States President and Army General Dwight D. Eisenhower. It uses importance and urgency as a tool to define priority. For example, items that are important and urgent are higher priority than items that are urgent but not important.

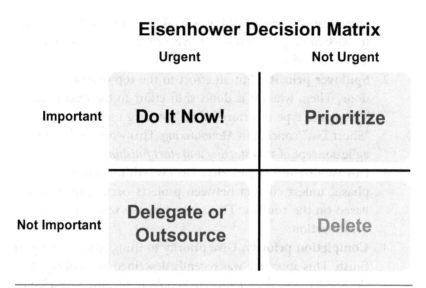

Figure 7.1   An Eisenhower Matrix.

Experiment

Problem: Backlogs are convenient dumping grounds for any request. Doing so is a form of waste for everyone involved.

Hypothesis: Backlogs should be as lean as possible. If an item isn't ever going to be done, delete it!

Do You Have This Problem?—Questions to Diagnose.

- How many iterations' worth of items are in the backlog? (Count the number of items in the backlog. Divide by the number of backlog items completed in a given amount of time.)
- What's the age of the oldest item in the backlog?
- Is the backlog prioritized?

Experiment: Plot your stories or features on the quadrants of the Eisenhower Matrix. For each item, decide which quadrant it belongs in. After all backlog items are in a quadrant, ask the following questions:

- Are the urgent/important items at the top of the backlog?
- Are the not urgent/important items in the middle/end of the backlog?

continued

- Are the urgent/not important items candidates to give to another team or group?
- Are the not urgent/not important items candidates for removal from the backlog?

Validation: Running the experiment should result in a prioritized backlog. It should also result in items flagged for removal. If the backlog doesn't get smaller after this experiment, try doing it again.

Example: A team decides to plot backlog items on the Eisenhower Matrix. They book a conference room and print out the backlog items from their electronic tool. The Scrum Master draws a version of the matrix on the whiteboard. The team members are each given a few items from the backlog and place them on the board. The Scrum Master walks through the items. The team and product owner have the opportunity to move them around. Afterward, the product owner adjusts the backlog to reflect the group's decisions.

Paul Spicker's "What is a priority?"[6] outlines a third approach to defining and assessing priority. The paper suggests five kinds of priorities:

1. **Priority as importance:** One item is more important than something else. Implementation of the word *important* is a matter of context and biases.
2. **Relative priority:** Importance is like weights that get distributed between options. The outcome is a decision on the priority of an item.
3. **Precedence:** The basis of priority is whether one option has to come before another option.
4. **Priority as special status:** Specific attributes influence priority. Set-asides are a form of special status. Tom worked with a firm where technical debt reduction had to be a set percentage. It had special status. In many organizations, specific products have special status. They are the first priority for people.

---

[6] Spicker, Paul. "What is a priority?" in *Journal of Health Services Research & Policy*, vol. 14, no. 2, 2009, pp. 112–116. (Downloaded 8/10/2021).

5. **Lexical ordering:** The order of items imputes priority. In the same organization, user interface/user experience was first on the priority list because it affected users. Lexical ordering is often influenced by other factors such as special statuses.

Spicker approached defining priority in a medical setting. Yet, the construct is useful for defining how we can create a framework for knowing what to do next.

Experience Report

Establishing a Common Definition of *priority*

The larger the group, the harder it can be to establish a common definition of priority. It's very easy for people and teams to diverge and create their own definition of what the term means. This is even more challenging when an organization is working toward a common goal—for example, let's say a product release. It can be hard establishing a linear "1 to n" list of priorities that all teams can follow. Yet, there is power in establishing the *number 1* priority for teams to rally around. In our experience, a type of work is easier to rally around. This can be something internal that's breaking something—for example, an automated test failure. It can also be a critical item that can't miss the release window—for example, a critical customer enhancement or defect fix. A common definition of top priority leaves no question about what teams should be working on. It also gives teams the ability to use their own heuristics for prioritizing the rest of their list.

END-OF-CHAPTER QUESTIONS

Use the following to start a conversation about the contents of this chapter:

1. What's your preferred definition of the word *priority*? Why?
2. What definition do people in your team or organization use for *priority*? Why?

3. Describe a time where you suggested prioritizing something. What was the outcome? Why?
4. What work is a priority in your team? Your company?
5. Do the priorities of your team/company align with the work that is being prioritized?

8

THE WHO, WHEN, AND HOW
OF PRIORITIZATION

Learning Objectives—by the end of this chapter, you will be able to:
- Describe who participates in prioritization of work in software product organizations
- Describe when prioritization occurs
- Describe how prioritization occurs

Understanding the word *priority* and why we do it is only half of the prioritization equation. People have a huge part to play in the prioritization of any list of work. The timing of that prioritization matters, as well. We'll explore both of those topics in this chapter.

WHO PARTICIPATES IN PRIORITIZATION?

Having a practice or technique for prioritizing by itself is not enough. The right people with the right information are key to getting any list prioritized the right way. Asking the wrong people to prioritize a list can be almost as bad as never prioritizing the list at all. There are several common roles that participate in prioritization. Each role brings a different perspective to the priority of work. But they all must be willing to listen to other opinions. The categories of roles to include are:

- **Product**
    - □ People in this category articulate how the items on the list will impact the product's customer base. Roles include product manager and product owner.
- **Process**
    - □ People in this category fulfill the needs of the organization and team for structure. Roles include portfolio manager, project manager, program manager, agile coach, and Scrum Master. These roles must understand the urgency and importance of the priorities. They must also understand the execution approach. These roles will know, at a high level, whether the teams have the capacity and expertise to do the work. People in these roles will often provide facilitation for prioritization activities.
- **Management**
    - □ People in this category perform several functions in prioritization. Roles include executive, portfolio epic sponsor, director, senior manager, manager, and team lead. The bigger the backlog items, the higher the level of management involvement. People in this category should discuss priorities with an open mind. They should be eager to hear opinions from others about the priority of the work. More often, though, they come to the discussion with their own agenda.
- **Customers**
    - □ If the work getting prioritized is for internal use, include an internal *customer*. Accounting or HR functions are examples of internal customers. In some companies, external customers help prioritize work. A firm we worked with consults user groups to prioritize enhancements. In most cases, the product manager or product owner acts as a

proxy for the customer. Customers can articulate value and pain from the perspective of a user.

- **Technical**
    - □ People in this category help understand how large a piece of work is. They also determine technical feasibility. Roles include architects, technical leads, and other subject matter experts. A piece of work that requires years of innovation before it can begin might not be the top priority. Watch the body language of these people when you ask how large something might be. If they look like deer in headlights, it's a sign that the item isn't well-scoped or is a technical impossibility.

You Asked . . .

What do terms like *large* mean in software-related projects? Size is a way of conveying some combination of the following:

- The number of people involved in a piece of work
- The perceived level of effort to complete the work
- The complexity
- The number of boundaries the work will cut across
- How much is unknown
- How long it will take to deliver

Three approaches are generally used to convey size:

- **Relative size measures:** These use the measurer's perspective as a framework to assess size. These measures are much akin to stepping off a distance and declaring it to be so many yards or feet. The measure is relative to the size of the measurer's stride.
- **Functional size measures:** These assess size based on a set of rules focused on user-recognizable functionality. Most functional measures focus on sizing requests (and later deliveries).
- **Physical measures of size:** These count tangible *things*. Flow metrics are physical measures, which include counting flow items and flow time.

Each approach has value. Each approach has different rules and perspectives.

- **Sales, Marketing, Technical Support, Business Analysis, User Interface/User Experience**
  - ❑ Technical support roles are often overlooked. In product companies, these functions almost always have a seat at the table. These areas have frequent contact with existing and prospective customers. They have their literal fingers on the pulse. They should be able to speak to:
    - ○ The *pain* for one or many customers if an item drifts to the bottom of the list
    - ○ The potential for future sales revenue for the items high up the priority list (market knowledge)
    - ○ How the functionality on the list matches up with competitors (competitive intelligence)

    Some organizations funnel sales and marketing information through product management. Meanwhile, technical support gets information through other technical channels. This is a form of the *telephone game* which should be avoided at all costs.

You Asked . . .

What about including team members in prioritization discussions?
There are some scenarios where including team members in prioritization discussions makes sense. For example, let's say a team member has experience in an industry that will be served by the product. They might have first-hand perspective on which features would benefit customers. More often, though, including team members in prioritization discussions isn't worthwhile. We've seen situations where team members confuse priority with how sexy the work is. In those circumstances, the business/technical divide gets sharpened and the conversation devolves. This is a reflection of the wrong people involved, as well as poor facilitation. We prefer to make team members aware of the priority and the rationale for the priority, then let them play a role in the conversation around sequencing of work.

Two more notes on roles:

1. All roles bring different perspectives to the table. Different perspectives are only useful when heard. Everyone involved in prioritization is best served to listen and operate with an open mind.
2. You need the right people for the right prioritization event. For example, executives shouldn't get involved in prioritizing work at the team level. Every event needs scope and context when deciding who to involve.

Experiment

Problem: As organizations grow, layers form between customers and teams. These communication chains can often be detrimental to understanding actual customer needs. This can lead to delivering work that doesn't address customer needs. The result is waste or rework.

Hypothesis: The closer teams get to customers, the better they will be at delivering work that addresses customer needs.

Do You Have This Problem?—Questions to Diagnose.

- Do the people doing the work discuss customer needs based on first-hand knowledge?
- Do the names of specific customers ever come up in conversation? Are they ever listed on backlog items?
- How often do customers interface with the people doing the work?
- Is there a repository of knowledge on how customers use the product(s)?

Experiment: Pick an item out of the backlog that was a customer request. It can be a big item (feature) or a small item (story). It can also be a big customer or a small customer. Ask the following questions:

- Could the team talk to the customer about this piece of work?
- How many internal people would the team need to talk to before they could talk to the customer?

continued

- How could the team get feedback from the customer after they do the work?
- How long would it take for the team to get feedback from the customer?

Validation: Answers to the aforementioned questions will let you know how difficult it's going to be for the team to get closer to customers. Validation cannot happen until teams get better visibility into customer needs. The primary outcome is richer conversations around customer needs. Another desirable outcome is less wasted work.

Example: A team enters sprint planning with a few customer-facing items in their backlog. The product owner admits that he doesn't know how to prioritize one of the requests. The request doesn't seem clear. It's for a customer that spends a lot of money every year on the product. The team thinks it's a small task (less than a day). The team agrees to do the item in the sprint. The product owner reaches out to some internal folks to get the name of a contact at the customer site. The Sprint Review invitation includes the name of the customer contact. During the Sprint Review, the team shows the backlog item to the customer. They verify that what they did is actually what the customer wanted.

WHEN TO PRIORITIZE

Prioritization differs from the old *timing is everything* axiom. There's never a time not to do it. Prioritization involves so much more than ordering a list of items in an electronic tool. Effective prioritization at all levels involves constant preparation, conversation, and synthesis. It is relentless.

People, teams, and firms that prioritize in a continuous way do so by building it into how they operate. They do not leave it to chance. For example, teams that use Scrum meet at the sprint boundary to discuss the plan for the next sprint. Part of that conversation involves the priority of items in the backlog. The product owner prioritizes the product backlog at the start of the sprint.

Refinement is an inextricable part of the prioritization process. As new work enters, people and teams examine it and determine how to solve a given challenge. That examination construes refinement. It can involve things like defining outcomes (acceptance criteria) or providing an estimate. The information that comes out of refinement can impact prioritization.

Backlog Health

The concept of backlog health is an important topic. This metric provides visibility into how much ready work a team has in front of them before their backlog runs dry. Backlog health is a simple calculation. Take the quantity of ready work in the backlog and divide it by typical flow velocity (throughput). For example, a team has 10 ready items in the backlog. They average five items done per week. Thus, they have a backlog health of two weeks. In our experience, teams that track backlog health rarely forget to refine their backlog.

Backlog Health at All Three Levels

While backlog health is perceived as a tactical measure, it is also useful in the middle and organization levels. The math is the same, but the scale and focus are different. The measures are aggregated to multiple teams and features instead of one team and their individual backlog items. For example, an organization has a backlog of 20 features. The flow velocity of features for the entire organization averages 10 per quarter. In this example, the organization has about two quarter's (six month's) worth of work in its backlog. This quick forecasting is helpful when new features emerge. It allows the organization's leaders to have conversations about prioritization and delivery.

HOW TO PRIORITIZE

Good prioritization does not happen in a vacuum. It involves conversations and data-informed decision making. Conversations and gathering data take time. The amount of information needed to prioritize is debatable. The concern is that decision making will fall prey to analysis paralysis. This concept first appeared in one of Aesop's fables, *The*

Fox and the Cat.[7] Avoiding a proverbial (or literal) rabbit hole requires having an approach and guidelines. We would like to propose a simple heuristic that you can use to determine how much time to spend prioritizing an item. The time spent should be proportional to how difficult it would be to recover from a prioritization mistake.

Let's look at two example scenarios:

- **Example:** A product owner is prioritizing stories for the next two-week sprint. There are 40 items in the backlog and the median flow velocity for the team is 10 items.
    - *Recommendation:* The product owner should prioritize 15 items. We arrived at this number by multiplying the median flow velocity of the team by 1.5 (the number of sprints for which we want to ensure we have enough items; the idea is to make sure you're prioritizing enough for the current sprint, as well as a little bit more in case the team finishes the work early and can pull more work, or needs to adjust the plan during the sprint). The product owner should spend no more than one hour prioritizing this work. We arrived at this number using 30 minutes per week in the planning period. The worst-case scenario is that the product owner picks the 10 lowest-value items for the next sprint. If this occurs, the product owner will hear about this at some point during the next two weeks. They will end up reprioritizing the list based on feedback. Weighing items in the product backlog like *The Thinker* isn't going to prove a useful exercise. The worst-case scenario isn't that bad.
- **Example:** A CEO is prioritizing large-scale initiatives that will cut across the company. There are four items to prioritize. These large-scale initiatives will take years of work. They will yield

---

[7] "The Fox and the Cat." Wikipedia, 10/2/2022, en.wikipedia.org/wiki/The_Fox_and _the_Cat_(fable).

iterative and incremental releases before they're mature products. The item that ends up at the top of the list will become the sole priority for the company for a long period of time.

- ☐ *Recommendation*: Spending a significant amount of time to curate this list of priorities makes sense. The worst-case scenario could prove catastrophic for the company. A true heuristic is difficult for this scenario. Organizations often spend lots of time doing strategic planning before committing.

Facilitating prioritization requires differing approaches and amounts of time. It depends on how impactful the items on the backlog are (see Table 8.1). Item size corresponds to the facilitation techniques you should use to prioritize.

Some thoughts on how to facilitate prioritization:

- Capture the rationale for decisions. At the team level, some light notes on a story card should suffice. At the organization and middle levels, do something more powerful. Consider a video recording or transcript of the decision-making event.
- There are many different techniques for prioritizing backlog items. Many are a variation of Donald Reinertsen's "cost of delay" (from *The Principles of Product Development Flow*[8]). The simplest version of cost of delay compares business value to job size and expresses it as a ratio. Business value and job size use the modified Fibonacci sequence that's taken root in the agile space over the last twenty years. Reinertsen's guidance is to find items that have a business value that's greater than their job size. For example, a piece of work has a business value of 20 and a job size of 1. The ratio is 20:1 (20). That means the piece of work will deliver a huge amount of business value in a minimal

---

[8] Reinertsen, Donald G. *The Principles of Product Development Flow: Second Generation Lean Product Development*, Celeritas Publishing, Redondo Beach, CA, 2009.

Table 8.1 Facilitation Techniques for Different-Sized Items

Level	General Perspective	Facilitation Techniques to Employ	Rationale
Organization	Decisions that impact large portions of the organization. They often appear quick but include significant analysis before prioritization events.	*Big room* events Corporate retreats Workshops	Communication about large items should be as synchronous as possible. Undivided attention helps prioritization happen more quickly.
Middle	The middle balances the needs and wishes of the levels above and below. At the same time, people at this level negotiate with their peers for work, people, and resources. This requires syncing strategic and long-term work with tactical and short-term.	Conference calls Workshops	Synchronous communication is most effective at this level. The difference between this level and the organizational level is considerable. In most cases, prioritization happens in iterations. This leaves less time for analysis. Prioritization on a cadence reduces the impact of making prioritization mistakes.
Team	Prioritization is easy because the number of degrees of freedom is smaller.	1:1 Conversations (in real life and virtual) E-mail	We recommend using the most intimate approach to prioritization that makes sense. Meeting face-to-face is more intimate than updating spreadsheets. However, prioritizing less impactful items can happen using e-mail. At the team level, the biggest impact of misprioritization is the impact on trust. A team will lose confidence in a product owner who gets prioritization wrong.

amount of time. The *cost of delay* of doing this work is likely quite high—both for the company and also the customers.

- Cost of delay activities lend themselves very well to discussions with diverse groups. Weighing the business value and the job size of items can yield rich conversations. They can yield a degree of empathy and alignment that few other techniques can hope to achieve.

END-OF-CHAPTER QUESTIONS

Use the following to start a conversation about the contents of this chapter:

1. Who participates in prioritization of work in your team or organization? Why?
2. How often does prioritization happen?
3. How is prioritization facilitated in teams? How is it done across the organization?
4. How often do priorities change?
5. Who makes changes in priorities?

9

PRIORITIZATION AT ALL
THREE LEVELS

Learning Objectives—by the end of this chapter, you will be able to:
- ▸ Describe traits of prioritization at all three levels—organization, middle, and team
- ▸ Describe the relationship between prioritization and work intake
- ▸ Describe simple and more complicated methods to prioritize a list of work

Prioritization at all three levels looks similar on the surface (see Table 9.1). This is because they support the same attributes. Yet, the level of granularity and specificity can be very different.

The priorities of each level include a mix of work. The level of granularity in the mix and measurement changes at each level of the organization. For example, the organization may specify a goal of 30 percent of work toward enhancements to current products. The team then prioritizes specific enhancements.

Table 9.1   Prioritization Attributes at All Levels

Priorities . . .	Organization	Middle	Team
Are explicit	X	X	X
Include a mix of work (i.e., enhancements and maintenance)	X (High level)	X	X (Specific)
Tie directly to company vision and strategy	X	X	1
Evolve to reflect customer and business needs	X	X	X
Are mentioned in Annual Shareholder Report	X	2	2

1: The connection between team-level priorities and strategic goals is often loose. Teams interpret these goals through the tactical lens of delivering and supporting products.

2: Middle management and teams prioritize support of specific strategies. These are not reflected in shareholder communication.

PRIORITIZATION AND WORK INTAKE

Prioritization is a critical component of a work intake strategy. Prioritization answers the question of which *items* to deliver and in what order. A simple, but solid, prioritization process includes:

- A transparent and unambiguous definition of what priority means
- An approach to applying that definition, in order to generate a list (or lists) in ranked order
- An approach for allocating the resources, people, and attention that the organization has available

Most definitions of priority convey *importance* and *an order of precedence*. This means doing the more important things before doing the less important things. This definition fits well with Merriam-Webster. It gets a bit iffy once work gets refined, planned, and the real world gets involved. The order in which work begins reflects the initial priority. This is some mix of prioritization and cheating (jumping the queue).

The real priority shows up more in the order that the work gets completed. Duration matters in the work intake equation. Getting something done is the ultimate expression of importance. As noted earlier, the term *important* is ambiguous. Unless defined in explicit terms, it is a reflection of some mashup of personal biases.

EXAMPLES OF A SIMPLE AND COMPLEX APPROACH TO PRIORITIZATION

A Simple—But Rigorous—Approach to Prioritization

There are many ways to execute even a simple definition of priority. The following text describes an example of a three-step approach.

Step One: Defining Importance

Importance needs anchoring in the strategic and tactical goals of the organization. If those goals are glittering generalities, reframe the goal(s) into something tangible. Some potential attributes are listed in Table 9.2.

All of these are solid, measurable attributes for gauging importance. The less ambiguous you can make the attributes of importance, the better. It will be easier to communicate with stakeholders when coming to a consensus.

Combining attributes to generate importance requires agreement on some form of relative weighting. Relative weighting often becomes a deterministic system that does not respect nuance. A modicum of human intuition and intervention is useful—especially during times when trends are ambiguous.

Step Two: Using the Classic Importance/Urgency Matrix

Planning tools, spreadsheets, and visualization tools help translate importance and urgency into priority. The Eisenhower Matrix, introduced in Chapter 7, is one example. It's a four-box matrix to visualize

Table 9.2   Attributes of Importance

Attribute	Example Definition	Example Goal
Customer Experience	Improve the feelings of customers and channel support toward the application.	Reduce the number of screens between starting an order and final submit.
Customer Care	Improve customer service to build a better relationship with customers.	Reduce customer wait times for customer service.
Client Outcomes	Improve the perception of whether the service satisfies the client's demonstrable expectations.	Double the number of referenceable clients for product X during the current fiscal year.
Quality	Improve performance against industry standard(s) used to measure the product.	Increase application uptime to 97% outside of service windows.
Cost Reduction	Reduce the overall cost of supporting, delivering, and enhancing the product.	Reduce product support costs by 10% in the current fiscal year.
Market Share	Increase the portion of the market owned by the product.	Increase the penetration of product usage in Fortune 50 firms.
Revenue Enhancement	Increase the top-line revenue delivered by the product.	Increase sales of product X by 10% in the current fiscal year.

the relationship between importance and urgency. The goal of the matrix is to show everyone the work that is both important and urgent. This approach also serves to highlight items that are not very important and not very urgent.

There are all sorts of variations on the Eisenhower Matrix. There's an expanded version with a total of nine boxes. This helps get more granular with visualizing priorities. Defining what each box means increases the up-front cost of using this approach. It pays off when organizations have a large portfolio of work for prioritizing.

Step Three: Allocating Work

Developing a priority list is an excellent first step toward meeting organizational goals. The next step in the process is to adopt a queueing approach. *Monotasking*[9] suggests doing one thing until it's done—with focused effort. Then, shift money to the next priority. The idea of monotasking is important for tasks and projects. In larger organizations, there are often independent streams of work (value streams). These streams can all use monotasking at the same time. Regardless of approach, everyone needs to understand and respect the priority queue. Without an approach for taking work into a team, chaos emerges. The most common antipattern is to start everything and try to keep as many proverbial balls in the air as possible—until someone screams. The screaming reestablishes the priority list.

Conclusion

The way a team or organization prioritizes work does not have to be complicated—but it is rarely simple. It is far easier to assume that everyone understands words like important and urgent. It's also easy to assume that priority order equates to delivery order. Unless you define a process to arrive at these definitions, you will never be sure that everyone is on the same page. One last piece of advice—make prioritization only as complicated as it needs to be and no more.

A More Complicated Approach to Prioritization: Weighted Shortest Job First

Not all prioritization exercises are simple techniques. Should you tackle an item that has a large payback in the future or choose the item that gets done sooner, but has a lower payback? This decision is not a moot point. In addition, dealing with office politics requires a more formal process. This heavier process ensures the perception of equity.

---

[9] Nöteberg, Staffan. *Monotasking: How to Focus Your Mind, Be More Productive, and Improve Your Brain Health*, Racehorse, New York, NY, 2021.

Simple does not always work, which is why more complex prioritization approaches evolve. Weighted Shortest Job First (WSJF) is one of the more useful heavy approaches.

WSJF begins with quantifying the cost of delay (CoD). CoD is a method of placing a value on the waste that is inherent in delay. There are any number of factors that need to be considered when determining the CoD. These include wait times, inventory costs, opportunity costs, and risk. Duration is a weighting mechanism to differentiate between projects.

In *The Principles of Product Development Flow: Second Generation Lean Product Development*,[10] Donald Reinertsen provides an example of WSJF. The example shows that if the CoD is the same for two jobs, you should do the shortest job first. Doing the shortest job first avoids at least some CoD and delivers value sooner. You will find an example of CoD in Table 9.3.

In the previous example, doing work item A, then B, and then C—shortest *time to complete* to longest—incurs a $400 CoD. This is calculated in the following manner:

- Work Item A = $0 CoD
- Work Item B = $100 CoD (1 day to complete item A × $100)
- Work Item C = $300 CoD (3 days [1 day to complete item A and 2 days to complete item B] × $100).

Table 9.3   Cost of Delay Example

	CoD (Per Day)	Time to Complete (Job Duration)
Work Item A	$100	1 Day
Work Item B	$100	2 Days
Work Item C	$100	5 Days

---

[10] Reinertsen, Donald G. *The Principles of Product Development Flow: Second Generation Lean Product Development*, Celeritas Publishing, Redondo Beach, CA, 2009.

Alternatively, doing the previously mentioned work items in the opposite order—longest *time to complete* to shortest—incurs a $1,200 CoD:

- Work Item C = $0 CoD
- Work Item B = $500 CoD (5 days × $100)
- Work Item A = $700 CoD (7 days [5 days to complete item C and 2 days to complete item B] × $100)

Doing the items from shortest to longest incurs a different CoD than the opposite order.

Things get messier when we combine estimates of CoD and *time to complete* to get a more granular picture. The Scaled Agile Framework (SAFe®)[11] uses CoD divided by duration to generate the weighted shortest job. The highest weighted shortest job gets done first. The calculation for WSJF (see Table 9.4) is CoD divided by duration.

The higher the WSJF, the sooner the work should be done. In the previous example, WSJF tells us that the most optimal order of completion would be work item C, then work item A, and then work item B. The total CoD accrued would be $2,428.

Table 9.4   CoD Example with WSJF

	CoD (Per Day)	Time to Complete (Job Duration)	Weighted Shortest Job
Work Item A	$100	25 Days	4
Work Item B	$75	30 Days	2.5
Work Item C	$600	3 Days	200

---

[11] "Weighted Shortest Job First." Scaled Agile Framework, 7/19/2023, www.scaledagileframework.com/wsjf/.

You Asked . . .

Doesn't WSJF favor small pieces of work? Yes. Duration has an outsized bearing in WSJF. WSJF forces stakeholders to streamline chunks of potential value to improve delivery flow.

WSJF is all about doing—and finishing—the *shortest job first*. Jobs get weighted by value. This is why duration—or *time to complete*—is the denominator in the CoD equation. Short jobs have to be valuable, though. Short jobs without value will not rise above those that are average in duration and value.

The realization that large chunks of value need to be *leaned down* rarely occurs at the start of a WSJF activity. It often occurs at the end, when stakeholders see the results. They realize that their highest priority isn't near the top of the list (i.e., has the highest WSJF score). They inspect the list and ask questions like, "How did that piece of work make it to number one?" Then they look at the math. Then they realize that they need to streamline the chunk of value that they brought to the WSJF activity.

When you use WSJF, don't expect stakeholder satisfaction with the final results. The dissatisfaction will be because their highest priority didn't make it to the top of the WSJF list. When facing this scenario, the correct outcome is to think smaller. Ask those unsatisfied stakeholders to streamline the proposed work. This will push it higher up the WSJF list the next time you conduct the WSJF activity. A less desirable outcome is to maintain the status quo. Both authors have seen stakeholders declare, "WSJF doesn't work for us, we know what our priorities are." Then they demand that the highest priority items get underway immediately.

Prioritization may be difficult for any number of reasons. These can range from perceiving differences between work items to political wrangling. As a result, there are a wide variety of techniques to approach prioritization. Assuming the validity of the approach, each exists to address different organizational constraints. WSJF addresses prioritization in complex scenarios. It does so by using the lean concept of CoD and duration/time to complete. This consistent economic framework is useful for complex portfolios. It is also useful where organizational politics requires control (but not confrontation). Consistency and repeatability means logic drives which work gets done in what order. Without a framework, it is often the squeaky wheel that gets the grease. Who knows whether or not that squeaky wheel will deliver the most value?

Experience Report

Using WSJF

WSJF is useful for collaborative prioritization of larger backlog items (features and epics). Conducting a WSJF session creates transparency. It exposes participants to the competition for resources. This is particularly true when explicit conversations about prioritization are rare. Without coaching and facilitation, participants will only bring some of the work to the session. The formality and coaching act as a forcing function to help expose *dark* work. We recommend maintaining and refining a pipeline for prioritization; this increases transparency. It also exposes when someone tries to slip something into the team's priorities.

Facilitating a WSJF activity is a great opportunity for stakeholders to connect. It gets them aligned with the work on the horizon. It also connects stakeholders in different areas. Jeremy was working with a set of teams supporting a general-purpose product. This product spanned different industries, such as healthcare, finance, and higher education. In the WSJF session, different stakeholders represented customer needs for each industry. During the session, everyone was able to speak for their industry, but most had little insight into customer needs in other industries.

The session was lengthy and involved some heated moments. The ultimate outcome was worth it. The session ended with a list of priorities that reflected the needs of every industry.

Steps to WSJF Facilitation

Facilitating a successful WSJF session involves a lot of moving parts. We have outlined a set of steps that we have taken to deliver successful WSJF sessions. The steps, the questions you will need to answer during each step, and guidance are included in the following sections.

Before the Session

1. **Identify participants**
   - Questions to answer
     - □ Which roles matter in prioritization and sequencing?
     - □ Which roles don't matter in prioritization and sequencing?
     - □ How much does hierarchy matter in prioritization and sequencing?
     - □ What's the highest level in the organizational chart that you need to include?
     - □ Which people can you exclude from the session and then later inform of the results?
     - □ Is everyone able to be in the same room for the activity or will you have to facilitate a hybrid session?
   - Guidance
     - □ Lots of people think their opinion matters in prioritization and sequencing. Include only those that matter and have a vested interest.
     - □ You, as facilitator, should have a good idea of whose opinions matter the most. Facilitate the conversation to make sure everyone hears them.
     - □ Consider who participates from all relevant/major functions in the company. Examples include development, sales, marketing, product management, etc.
     - □ Including more than one person from a function will weigh decisions toward that function.
     - □ Keep the participant list manageable—remember, the session should be a conversation.

2. **Determine timing**
   - Questions to answer
     - □ When is the right time to conduct the activity?
     - □ Are important stakeholders and participants available?
     - □ Are the WSJF results required for the next sprint, quarterly plan, yearly plan, etc.?

- Guidance
  - Do WSJF far enough in advance of a planning boundary so that it will be helpful input. Don't do it so far in front of the boundary that the results are stale. For example, if a program is doing quarterly planning, conduct WSJF around the middle of each quarter.

3. **Work in progress (WIP) inventory**
   - Questions to answer
     - What are the teams currently working on?
     - Will their current WIP impact the amount of work getting prioritized during the upcoming WSJF?
     - Should the current WIP be part of the WSJF?
     - What WIP will not get finished by the next boundary (sprint, quarter, etc.)? Should it carry forward past the next boundary?
   - Guidance
     - Starting and finishing work within committed boundaries is imperative when using WSJF. If the system is full of WIP, it's hard to gauge when new work from WSJF can enter. Clear the system of WIP before including work that comes out of WSJF.

4. **Refine new work**
   - Questions to answer
     - What is the backlog of items that will be part of WSJF?
     - Who is responsible for refining the backlog items?
     - How do we know when an item is ready for WSJF?
   - Guidance
     - This is the step that requires the most work in the run up to the WSJF session. Companies with a portfolio management process should leverage that to prepare backlog items for WSJF. Companies that don't have this process will need to stand up something on an ad hoc basis to make WSJF happen.

> ☐ This step is the *prioritization before the prioritization*. Stakeholders have to limit and prioritize their list of items.
>
> ☐ Establish a *definition of ready* for WSJF. This should include: description, acceptance criteria, customer impact, revenue implication, and affected team(s).

5. **Pick tools/location**
   - Questions to answer
     - ☐ What tools will you use to facilitate the session?
     - ☐ Will the session include remote participants?
     - ☐ Do you need to book a meeting room or off-site location?
     - ☐ Will anyone help you facilitate?
   - Guidance
     - ☐ Hybrid sessions are hard to pull off. Get everyone in the same room or do it remotely.
     - ☐ Consider doing WSJF at an off-site location to promote engagement and minimize multitasking.

6. **Set the rules**
   - Questions to answer
     - ☐ Will you be following Reinertsen's WSJF approach or will you be following the WSJF approach outlined in SAFe® (or some hybrid)?
     - ☐ What is your plan to train people on the rules? Will you send out a training document to be read before the session or use part of the session to train people?
     - ☐ What are the time boxes you will be following?
   - Guidance
     - ☐ Let participants know the rules before the session. Expect that you will always need to spend some time during the session to train.
     - ☐ Make sure everyone understands CoD before starting the session. Put the definition in a prominent location—for example, on a flip chart in the front

of the room or on the whiteboard if the session is remote.

During the Session

1. **Be on time**
   - Guidance
     - Keep the session *on track* by observing the time boxes. WSJF sessions are full of conversations. Keep in mind that not all are relevant.
     - Don't be afraid to cut off the conversation with questions like, "How does this impact the score for this item?"
2. **Capture actions**
   - Guidance
     - The outcome of WSJF is a list of work with corresponding scores. Other actions will crop up. Those could include further refinement of a WSJF item. It could also include creation of new backlog items or staffing actions.
     - Keep track of actions on sticky notes or in a shared document repository. Read out the action items at the end of the session.
3. **Facilitate**
   - Guidance
     - We've had success using the SAFe® approach to WSJF. That approach involves running the same list of work through four sets of questions. Use the modified Fibonacci scale as the scale.
     - When facilitating WSJF, answer the same question for each item. Then, move to the next question, and repeat for all items. For example, do the *user-business value* questions for all items, then move on to *time criticality*. This promotes consistent thinking and measuring items against each other.

After the Session

1. **Disseminate results and actions**
   - Questions to answer
     - ☐ What is the process for following up on actions?
     - ☐ Who do you need to inform about action-item resolutions?
     - ☐ When is the next WSJF?
   - Guidance
     - ☐ Send out the results and actions to participants and other interested parties.
     - ☐ If you have identified when the next WSJF session will take place, get it on the calendar. If not, determine when it will take place.

END-OF-CHAPTER QUESTIONS

Use the following to start a conversation about the contents of this chapter:

1. How is prioritization across all three levels similar? How does it differ?
2. How does prioritization relate to work intake?
3. What methods have you used to prioritize a list of work?
4. How do changes in priorities impact your team and workload?
5. How are priorities and changes communicated to the team?
6. How do changes in priorities impact the WIP?

10

PRIORITIZATION ANTIPATTERNS

> **Learning Objectives**—by the end of this chapter, you will be
> able to:
> - Recognize prioritization antipatterns
> - Effectively resolve prioritization antipatterns

Let's examine some phrases that get bandied about during discussions of priority. We'll repeat the phrase, describe the context, and then suggest how to react when—and it will be *when*—you encounter it.

"I CAN'T PRIORITIZE BETWEEN THESE ITEMS."

This phrase calls to mind the story of King Solomon and the baby. Instead of picking the true mother, King Solomon offered to divide the baby in half. In the context of prioritization, this phrase screams, "I can't choose the most important thing. So, I'll choose nothing!" The ramifications of this kind of phraseology can be opposite ends of the spectrum. It can yield complete paralysis because nobody knows what to work on—or it can yield a complete work in progress (WIP) fest because everything is important.

The reality is that we humans prioritize things every day. We call it *making decisions*. This morning, Jeremy chose to go for a run. Said another way, he prioritized running over a myriad of other things he could have done with his time. When he got home, he decided to do some yoga. He prioritized yoga ahead of things like eating a meal.

What should you do, then, if you hear a product owner or a manager tell you that they can't prioritize? Well, you could educate them on the fact that they make priority decisions every day—and then scold them for not being able to do that at work. But that doesn't seem like a great way to win friends and influence people.

Try these antipattern antidotes:

- **"Why can't you prioritize?"** This could be the start of a 5 *Whys* type of root cause analysis to try and identify what's going on here. This could yield a very positive response. But it could also yield the familiar parental response: "Because."
- **"What do you need to be able to prioritize?"** This is a much more effective and powerful question. It does presuppose that the person(s) wants to prioritize the work, but they're unable to for some reason. They could be missing information that would help inform the prioritization decision. The information could be there but not visible. They could need approval from someone else to even be able to prioritize. They could also not know what they need to be able to prioritize. If that's the case, this question will open the door to continuing the conversation.
- **"Can we prioritize in buckets?"** When many people think of prioritization, they think of a linear list. "This is first, this is second, this is third," etc. In the real world, though, priorities aren't often that clear. This is particularly true when you're establishing a priority list for a group of people. If there's a true *number one* priority, that's great. But it might only get worked on by a few members of the group. What about everyone else? Do they sit around and wait on that item to finish? Doubtful. Don't get hung up on a prioritized linear list. Focus on getting items into

buckets (e.g., high, medium, and low). This activity reduces the effort to prioritize. It brings clarity to what items are competing with one another for attention. If you still crave a linear list after grouping items in buckets, go right ahead. Give linear priority to the items within each bucket.

"THAT'S A HIGH PRIORITY."

The only thing worse than an inability to prioritize is the opposite end of the spectrum. It's the sentiment that everything is important and urgent. Not everything we do is a high priority, nor is it deserving of the high priority label. Jeremy went for a run this morning, but he didn't get out of bed thinking that his highest priority was exercise. He allocates time in his day to run and it almost always ends up being first thing in the morning. It's an enabler to his day; something he does to feel like he starts the day off on the right foot. Running might be one of the things he does first every day, but it's not something he considers a *high priority*. If he weren't able to run for a few days or weeks, he'd miss it, but his world wouldn't cease to exist.

Using our real-world lens, let's deconstruct the phrase that's the title of this section. As professionals, some of us get motivated by the prospect of doing work that will change the world. Meaningful work fuels the intrinsic motivation of knowledge workers. We'd much rather come to work thinking that the products we're building might change the world in some small (or big) way. It's much better than spending countless hours working on something that may not ever get used.

Try these antipattern antidotes:

- **"To whom is it a high priority?"** This question forces thinking in broader terms. There are implications to reacting to every request like it's the end of the world. Is it a high priority because it's promised to a customer? Is it a high priority because it's part of a C-level's pet project? Is it a high priority because it enables a future piece of work that's important? Use the Eisenhower Matrix to determine where the request belongs.

- **"If we had to prioritize work in a linear fashion, where would this item go?"** This question can shift the paradigm of a conversation or even the nature of an entire backlog. This question is most effective when the backlog is already prioritized in buckets (e.g., low, medium, and high priority). We've seen bucket-izing work as an effective approach to get a handle on a large backlog. This is particularly true when there is a need for backlog remediation. While bucket-izing is a valid way to prioritize, it presents opportunities for dysfunction. We've seen backlogs of work where every item has the high priority label on it ("everything is important!"). We've also seen backlogs look the complete opposite. Many items are low priority, and there are few items in the medium and high buckets ("most of this backlog is useless"). This can be an indicator of deeper issues. One is funding/allocation of people ("why are we funding this team of people?"). Another is the product owner ("is the person filling this role unable to find meaningful work for the team to do?"). In either case, prune backlogs that are full of low priority work—or delete them altogether.

"WHAT IS THE NEXT THING ON THE PRIORITY LIST?"

This question crops up when people and/or teams aren't quite sure what to do after they've finished a piece of work. When people are not sure what to do next, they will often ignore the backlog and go looking for work. As a form of rationalization, they may ask themselves:

1. Should I take the next item off the top of the list?
2. Should I ask someone what to focus on next?
3. Is there an incoming request that I need to address?
4. Can I help other team members finish their work?

Asking question number three instead of the others is a work intake faux pas. Instead, ask what is the next thing on the priority list (or have someone else ask the question). Regardless of who asks the question, the first response should be to open up the priority list. Having this list displayed brings context to the conversation you're about to have.

Try these antipattern antidotes:

- **"When was the last time this list was updated?"** This question ensures that the list is up-to-date with the current information. Depending on the size of the items, the priority may not have been updated for weeks or months. Always make sure the work at the top of the backlog is ready to go. If anyone has to wait for work to get refined, they will find something else to do (another work intake faux pas).

- **"How is this list prioritized?"** This question gives team members the opportunity to reinforce the priority rationale.

- **"How can we make priorities obvious?"** Making priorities explicit is something that many effective agile teams practice early on. In Scrum, the product owner makes priorities explicit. They do so by ordering the backlog in a way that makes the priorities evident to both those inside and outside the team. The question is an indicator that priorities are not as explicit as people are being led to believe. This question can also mean that people don't have access to the backlog, which is a huge transparency problem. The question suggests some ambiguity. Even if there aren't obvious issues with backlog prioritization, explore the issue—the conversation may yield ideas for improvement.

- **"Is there anything we know about that isn't on this list?"** This question opens the floor for people to bring new items up for prioritization. Is anyone already working on something that is not on the list? Is there a new request that might be urgent? Do we have ideas for the product that we have not yet captured as items? The goal of this question is not to shift into full-on backlog refinement mode or to inject work into the system. Instead, the question honors the need for total visibility into the work that is in front of a group of people. Get everything on the list.

"EVERYTHING IS A HIGH PRIORITY."

If you are lucky, you will only hear this phrase in times of extreme pressure—for example, the final push before some sort of delivery. If you are unlucky and hear it more often, we recommend changing jobs. "Everything is a high priority" can take two different tones. The first is one of unbridled cynicism. Think of a tenured employee giving a history lesson on how prioritization works (or doesn't). The second is the complete opposite—a tone of absolute seriousness. Think about a project manager checking in with a team to discuss the items on their board. No matter which one of these two tones is used to deliver this sentence, neither one is ideal. The cynical tone belies a sense of truth (and ambivalence), while the serious tone betrays a sense of ignorance.

The phrase "everything is a high priority" can cause one of two reactions. The first is *priority paralysis*. This occurs when a group that is trained to only follow a prioritized list hears this statement. They have no idea what to do, so they freeze. It might take a few minutes or a few business days to thaw. The second reaction is the complete opposite—excessive WIP. People or teams begin to think they'll get a reward for starting something. This thought process has a distinct look. "It's all high priority, so why not grab an item and work on it until the next interesting thing comes in? That new thing will be high priority, too, so it only makes sense to switch to that item. And then, if I get bored with that one, there will be a new item to look at—or I can switch back to the first item." Excessive WIP is a work intake failure that generates neglected WIP. The outcome is slower throughput with less value delivered.

Try these antipattern antidotes:

- **Open up the priority list.** This will prove whether this statement is actually true. If items have distinct priorities, this statement is being used to instill a sense of urgency. If everything has the same priority, shift the conversation. Make *priority* synonymous with *closest to done*. The item that is closest to done gets the mantle for highest priority. That's the item that the group needs to rally behind to finish. The item that's next closest *to done* is the next highest priority, etc.

- **Take a look at WIP.** Are there WIP limits? Are WIP limits respected or exceeded? How many people are on the team? Does the quantity of items in progress surpass the number of people on the team? One metric that can be helpful in this context is that of neglected WIP. To calculate neglected WIP, take the current WIP and subtract the predicted WIP. After calculating neglected WIP, show it to the team. Ask the team to refrain from starting anything new until the system clears the excessive WIP. (That is, unless the system is down or health and human safety is at risk.) Shift prioritization to focus on what is closest to done. Ignore what is deemed most important. Reinforce that customers buy products that are *done*. Customers don't pay for WIP.

PRIORITIZATION ANTIPATTERNS CONCLUSION

Priority is a word that is easy to say, but is often difficult to apply with equity and consistency. Almost everyone would agree that determining what is important is, well—important. Very few people want to spend the time *doing* formal prioritization. The shortcut of trusting your gut takes far less time and mental effort. Winging the prioritization process shows that individuals or organizations have forgotten the importance of conversations. The mere act of prioritization is a worthwhile activity. It connects and aligns people all along the value chain.

A final thought on prioritization; we have worked with teams who were laser focused on getting prioritization perfect. We have seen Weighted Shortest Job First activities that included razor-thin margins and lots of decimal points. We have worked with product owners who rank ordered backlog items for a whole year of work. Prioritizing a list of work is all about the outcome you're trying to achieve—not the math or the tool you're using. Don't get hung up on perfection before starting the conversation about prioritization.

END-OF-CHAPTER QUESTIONS

Use the following to start a conversation about the contents of this chapter:

1. Which of the prioritization antipatterns in this section have you experienced? What were the circumstances? How did you solve them?
2. What other prioritization antipatterns have you seen? What were the circumstances? How did you solve them?

11

SEQUENCING

Learning Objectives—by the end of this chapter, you will be able to:
> Define the word *sequencing*
> Describe why sequencing takes place
> Describe what sequencing is

Deciding the order in which to do pieces of work can be both a dynamic and an elusive process. The more complex the organization and its product line, the more complex it will be to lay out the order of things. For companies that operate in silos, this challenge grows exponentially. Like prioritization, continual communication and conversation are key to sequencing.

We thought long and hard about whether we had read about the topic of sequencing in any of our favorite agile texts. We both drew a blank. It is a topic that doesn't show up very often, and we are not sure why. In our experience, sequencing is a fundamental aspect of organizational agility.

WHY WE SEQUENCE

Work that has predecessors and/or successors—dependencies—requires sequencing. This allows work to get done in an efficient manner that reduces waste (aka, *stuff sitting around*). In agile, sequencing enables self-organization. It provides visibility into what it is going to take to get work that the business wants done. Even if every piece of work was independent from each other, sequencing would still have to happen. This is because doing work involves people. Effective sequencing combines technical construction requirements, capabilities of teams and organizations, and priority. This determines the order in which work gets queued up and started. Sequencing is fluid. Priorities change, capabilities change, and solutions to problems change.

From a logistics perspective, sequencing:

- **Occurs most often at boundaries**—for example, sprints, program increment planning, quarters, and budgeting events
- **Reacts to business and technical context**—sequencing translates the vision established by priorities into action
- **Is affected every time a person decides to start a piece of work**—especially if work happens out of order

Sequencing and Cross-Functional and Cross-Disciplinary Teams

Sequencing is a way for teams to plan to get work done. Regardless of whether cross-functional or cross-disciplinary teams or team members exist. A cross-functional team has the skills to get a piece of work done within the team; for example, when developers and testers are on the same team. A cross-disciplinary team has the ability to work across disciplines; for example, when hardware engineers and firmware engineers are on the same team.

Can a team be both cross-functional and cross-disciplined? Yes! Have we ever seen this in practice? Yes! Have either of us seen it often? No! Exclamations aside, cross-functional teams tend to be the more common agile teaming model. Regardless of the type of teaming model, team stability must happen. This gives the team the ability to learn enough to be cross-functional. The idea of a cross-disciplinary team that supports multiple products/packages is interesting. Unfortunately, it is rarely attainable.

Two attributes of work have a huge impact on the need for sequencing. The first is cohesion. This is the strength of the relationship between components in the system. The second is the level of independence between work items. Work items that are cohesive and lack independence must get done all together. They also have to get done in a specific order, or they will fail to meet their objective. In this scenario, sequencing the work is a must.

WHAT IS SEQUENCING?

Sequencing is deciding on the order in which work gets done. All processes have an explicit or implicit sequence. One step may have more value; yet, all the other parts enable that value. A simple example would be brushing your teeth. You pick up the brush, put toothpaste on it, brush, and clean up. In this example, there is no value until you have clean teeth. But if you didn't put toothpaste on the brush, your teeth wouldn't get cleaned, demonstrating that the sequence is important. Examples of sequence in the workplace include:

- **Product roadmap:** Almost every product firm has a product roadmap. This roadmap portrays how a product will change over time. That vision reflects both prioritization and sequencing.
- **Architectural runway:** The Scaled Agile Framework describes architectural runway as "consisting of the existing code, components, and technical infrastructure needed to implement near-term features."[12] This is a form of sequencing.

Sequencing is not only about figuring out the order in which work will get done. A well-sequenced plan takes into account the work of other

---

[12] "Architectural Runway." Scaled Agile Framework, 7/19/2023, scaledagileframework .com/architectural-runway/.

disciplines in the value chain; for example, the research, user interface/ user experience, and automation work that is related to the work that the teams are doing. Another example is the training and marketing that happens after the work is finished.

END-OF-CHAPTER QUESTIONS

Use the following to start a conversation about the contents of this chapter:

1. How often is the word sequencing used in your context?
2. What examples of sequencing have you recently seen?
3. Which role in your company coordinates sequencing across multiple teams?
4. How often does sequencing change within your team?

12

THE WHO, WHEN, AND HOW OF SEQUENCING

Learning Objectives—by the end of this chapter, you will be able to:
- ▸ Describe who participates in sequencing work in software product organizations
- ▸ Describe when sequencing occurs
- ▸ Describe how sequencing occurs

WHO PARTICIPATES IN SEQUENCING?

Everyone in the value chain must have a part in sequencing. If people or functions get left out, there is a risk of bottlenecks slowing the delivery of value.

Where and when the sequencing is being done determines who participates in sequencing. At the organization level, the strategic perspective is imperative. The chief information officer/chief technology officer and product management are integral in sequencing at this level. Senior technical people should provide the perspective of what is possible. They should also provide perspective on what needs to happen first. At the team and middle levels, people who understand how to deliver work bring the knowledge. They understand what needs to happen and in what order. Stakeholders from architecture and operations are also included—as are product and technical personnel from the relevant functional areas.

When large initiatives get decomposed, there are changes as to which people are involved in sequencing. Roles with strategic perspectives do strategic-level sequencing. Roles with tactical perspective participate when code is being written and hardware is constructed. The English have a saying—"horses for courses"—that alludes to the idea that a racehorse performs best on a track that is best suited to its capabilities. In sequencing, the best roles to involve are those who are involved in or are affected by the work.

WHEN TO SEQUENCE

Like prioritization, there is never a time not to keep sequencing in mind. Effective sequencing at all levels involves constant preparation, conversation, coordination, and synthesis. It is relentless, and it often spans large groups of people.

People, teams, and firms that sequence in a continuous way do so by building it into how they operate. They do not leave it to chance. Roles like technical project managers and technical program managers often facilitate these activities.

HOW TO SEQUENCE

Like prioritization, good sequencing does not happen in a vacuum. It involves conversations and data-informed decision making. So how much time should you invest in sequencing work? The time spent sequencing is proportional to the timescale for which you are sequencing work. Let's take a look at two examples:

- A team is sequencing stories in its product backlog for the next two-week sprint. There are 10 items in the backlog.
  - In this example, the worst-case scenario is that the team gets sequencing completely wrong. If this happens, the

team will discover their error at some point during the next two weeks. They will end up resequencing the work as soon as they realize their mistake. Agonizing over the sequencing of work for a short timescale is not worth it. During planning, discuss the cohesion and independence of the work.

- A team of architects is working with executives to sequence work for initiatives that will cut across the company. There are four items to sequence. Those four items will yield hundreds of smaller hunks of work that will also need sequencing. These initiatives entail years of iterative and incremental releases.
  - □ In this example, spending a significant amount of time sequencing initiatives is important. The outcome of sequencing initiatives is a roadmap. Roadmaps can demand weeks of effort to construct and refine. They need continuous refinement after the work begins. The worst-case scenario could prove catastrophic for the company. It could yield half-done products waiting on dependent work. These products could lack functionality and be out of date by the time they are done.

END-OF-CHAPTER QUESTIONS

Use the following to start a conversation about the contents of this chapter:

1. Who participates in sequencing work for your team or organization?
2. When does sequencing occur for your team or organization?
3. What is the process for sequencing work for your team or organization?

13

SEQUENCING AT ALL THREE LEVELS

> **Learning Objectives**—by the end of this chapter, you will be able to:
> - Describe traits of sequencing at all three levels—organization, middle, and team
> - Describe the relationship between sequencing and work intake
> - Describe how to approach sequencing a list of work

In a hierarchy, sequencing is a set of cascading decisions. As the ripples fan out, they get weaker and get influenced by other phenomena. Consider what happens when you throw a rock in a calm pond. Ripples fan out in pretty circles propagating far from the epicenter. Throw the same rock into a turbulent pond and the effect is far less pronounced and predictable. An organization with poor control over work intake is akin to a turbulent pond. The horizon that any decision can impact shrinks.

Here is what sequencing looks like at all three levels:

- **Organization:** Sequencing at this level reflects how work fits into the organization's goals and objectives. This is strategy in action. Budgets, money, people, capabilities, and resources all contribute to sequencing decisions. Organizational politics also play a big role.

- **Middle:** Sequencing at this level is the mushiest. This is because it balances and aligns tactical and strategic perspectives. It does this while under pressure from people who are not at the tactical or strategic table.
- **Team:** At the team level, sequencing becomes a technical discussion. Pertinent questions must be answered such as "What has to go first in order to be able to assemble something and deliver it?"

SEQUENCING AND WORK INTAKE

In some respects, sequencing is as important to work intake as prioritization. It's not good enough to know that something is important. You must translate that importance into something tangible. Sequencing is where the proverbial rubber meets the road.

APPROACH TO SEQUENCING

An effective approach to sequencing work requires knowledge of the following:

- **The capacity of the system:** Understanding the capacity of the system is essential. Is a team planning a sprint or is a program planning a longer time box? How else will you know how much work can get done?
- **The estimated size of the work:** This is another essential data point. Whether it's a story, a feature, or something bigger, you can understand the size of the work using flow metrics, function points, or story points. This data allows planning based on the capacity of the system. It helps answer the age-old question: "When will it be done?"

- **The skills required to do the work:** People do the work. Certain people (and teams) may be better equipped to do the work than other people (or teams). Matching people's skills to the work will influence the order of the work.
- **Dependencies between work items:** Sequencing is the order in which work gets done. Some work can happen in a concurrent fashion; some work cannot. Understanding what dependencies exist before work begins is a huge benefit to sequencing. Do not be content with the existence of the dependencies. Consider doing whatever possible to break them; for example, by upskilling a group of people so that they can do the work. Dependencies are often caused by organizational design.

Armed with the aforementioned approach, the next step is combining the work into a single view that includes a timescale. We have seen this done in electronic tools like Microsoft Excel or Mural. We have also seen this done with low-tech tools such as a whiteboard and sticky notes. The important part is to create the visual. This is because the visual is the backdrop for any conversation about the work. Visuals promote shared understanding and feedback in a way that talking rarely does. After work begins, we recommend keeping the sequencing visual updated. Use it for continued conversation about the work in progress.

END-OF-CHAPTER QUESTIONS

Use the following to start a conversation about the contents of this chapter:

1. How is sequencing across all three levels similar? How does it differ?
2. How does sequencing relate to work intake?
3. What methods have you used to sequence a list of work?

14

SEQUENCING ANTIPATTERNS

> **Learning Objectives**—by the end of this chapter, you will be able to:
> - Recognize sequencing antipatterns
> - Effectively resolve sequencing antipatterns

Let's examine phrases that get bandied about during sequencing discussions. We will talk about each phrase, as well as what you can do when you encounter each situation.

"THAT WORK ISN'T IN OUR BACKLOG OF PRODUCT WORK; IT'S IN OUR BACKLOG OF TECHNICAL WORK."

This antipattern is almost self-explanatory. It speaks to having two separate backlogs of work. One for product work (think user stories in a Scrum product backlog) and another backlog for technical enablement work (think deep technical items). Two backlogs may exist for any of the following reasons:

- Different people are responsible for prioritizing each backlog.
  - ❑ Someone with business context prioritizes the backlog of product work—they may or may not have any technical acumen. Someone with technical knowledge prioritizes the backlog of technical work—this is often a team member or architect.
- Different cadences of refinement may exist for each backlog.
  - ❑ When there are different backlogs, timing becomes an issue. The backlog of product work gets prioritized and refined in the run up to the release of the product. This is regardless of the release cadence. The backlog of technical work gets built up throughout the course of the release. It only gets refined when the team has the time to get to it. Technical backlog refinement and sequencing often happens after release. Alignment of the two backlogs is impossible—except through luck.

In both scenarios, the groups often don't recognize the need for sequencing all of the work together. Each group may see the other as lacking. The business people think the technical people don't have business understanding. The technical people think the business people don't have technical understanding. Having two backlogs is a recipe for disaster. Technical enablers and functional outputs need to be on the same list. This gives teams the ability to commit to delivering value without smoke and mirrors.

Try these antipattern antidotes:

- **"What product work does the technical work enable?"** One backlog is the correct solution, but demanding this will often only harden positions. Instead, start with some discovery work. Establish a clear connection between the two types of work. Everyone involved needs to understand that technical work enables the product work. If there isn't a clear connection, ask why the technical work is in the backlog. When you identify the connection, make it visible.

- **"Who prioritizes each backlog?"** This question is all about evaluating who is currently involved with each backlog. The answer identifies the people who must work together to combine the two backlogs.
- **"How often does each backlog get prioritized?"** This question helps to identify timing issues. Expect there to be a mismatch between how often each backlog gets prioritized.

These three questions are *discovery* questions. The goal is to combine both backlogs into one list of work. The trick is to do so without reverting to command-and-control tactics that will build more barriers than they resolve.

"THAT'S NOT ON OUR BACKLOG."

This antipattern often pops up after prioritization, sequencing, and planning. A request to do something else comes in, but work has started and it is too late to change course. "That's not on our backlog" can be a major impediment for everyone involved. Envision a scenario where a team identifies a need from another team. They don't need the item immediately, but will need it before the product is ready to ship. It is a clear dependency. A conversation happens between the teams. For whatever reason, the team that is the source of the dependency neglects to put the item in their backlog. When the team that needs the work checks in a few months later, the response is, of course, "That's not on our backlog."

Try these antipattern antidotes:

- **"Why not?"** This is the first question to ask in this scenario. And it is a question that might get asked with a sense of urgency. After all, "We needed it yesterday!" The goal of this question is not to accuse, but to understand where communication broke down. The hope is that it does not happen again.

- **"How can we get it on your backlog and prioritized?"** It is important to understand the full context of work intake at various levels. It's possible that this group has a different approach to managing work requests. They could have a different set of priorities or they could be working on things in a completely different sequence than you expected. The context is unknown. Understanding the context helps rectify the problem, now and in the future.

When a dependency shows up, build in a mechanism to follow up with, in order to avoid surprises. In many tools, there are ways to track work items as they move through their life cycles. *Use them.* That will ensure that no one has forgotten they have a commitment to meet.

"WE'RE GOING TO NEED TO DO THAT WORK EVENTUALLY, SO LET'S JUST DO IT NOW."

This antipattern is more subtle than some of the others in this chapter. On the surface, it reads like something that should definitely happen. A team is being proactive and doing work that they know they must do—whether it is product work or technical work. This mentality opens the door for lots of waste to creep into the value delivery process—whether it is value for external or internal customers. Consider what would happen if a team does work assuming one approach, then the design changes because of some emerging need. Other considerations include:

- The work that gets done isn't the right thing.
    - Mitigate this via frequent demonstrations and deliveries. The chance that it is the right thing degrades over time. In a best-case scenario, the work that got done is perfect. A more likely scenario is that further changes will have to happen at some point before delivery. In this scenario, changes result in context switching to revise the initial

work. In the worst-case scenario, the work is completely scrapped.

- Completing work with a higher cost of delay.
  □ The people doing the work put their own desires first. These end up being ahead of the prioritization and sequencing mechanisms that exist.

Try these antipattern antidotes:

- **"Do we understand the work?"** The reason to start here is that doing work out of order is often an assumption made in a vacuum. Assumptions without conversation and testing are ego traps—whether they are assumptions about users, teams, or technical challenges. Even if we assume good intentions, we have foregone the value of team decision making. Making these kinds of decisions may appear to be efficient, but the perception can get blown out of the water if the work that gets done is not the right work. Always begin by ensuring understanding. Having the backlog item visible during the discussion is important; it gets people to stop talking about what they think needs to happen. Instead, they start talking about what they are actually going to do. Often, the conversation that transpires is useful in helping better scope the work.
- **"When is the latest it is needed?"** It's great to assume it is needed, and it's easy to validate that assumption. But *when* it is needed can be a different story. The answer could be, "They need it next sprint." Asking this question could also cause someone to look at a roadmap and discover that the work isn't needed for years. This opens the door for the next question.
- **"Is there higher priority work we could be doing instead?"** Get clarity on the work and a potential timeline to complete, but always come back to priority. All teams minimize wasteful work by examining their list of priorities. Failure to do this—even with work that people think is high priority—is asking for waste to creep in.

END-OF-CHAPTER QUESTIONS

Use the following to start a conversation about the contents of this chapter:

1. Which of the sequencing antipatterns in this section have you experienced? What were the circumstances? How did you solve them?
2. What other sequencing antipatterns have you seen? What were the circumstances? How did you solve them?

15

PRIORITIZATION AND SEQUENCING—RELATED BUT DIFFERENT

> **Learning Objectives**—by the end of this chapter, you will be able to:
> - › Express how prioritization and sequencing differ
> - › Articulate why both sets of activities are required to efficiently deliver value

Prioritization and sequencing are both interrelated, yet very different:

- **Prioritization answers what work is the most important:** It is based on the weighting criteria of whoever is doing the prioritization. Examples include Weighted Shortest Job First and the Eisenhower Matrix.
- **Sequencing starts after prioritization occurs:** It takes the relative importance and then factors in how a group is going to make the work happen. Sequencing answers in what order that work must get done. It is based on technical and political rationale.

Priority influences sequencing; that is how they are interrelated. Priority is a higher-order construct. There is a one-too-many relationship between prioritization and sequencing. One thing gets prioritized and many things get sequenced. Think about the interaction between common agile roles, such as a product owner and a team. A product owner cares about value established through goals and priorities. The team translates that into action via sequencing. Sprint planning can be more of a sequencing conversation than a planning conversation. In a perfect world, prioritization and sequencing would be the same. The right person would be in the right place at the right time—all the time. But as we all know; we do not live in a perfect world.

Here is a simple example of the difference between prioritization and sequencing. In your list of daily priorities, getting to the office on time is a high priority. There is a long list of things that need to happen to get you to the office on time, though. Determining the order of those tasks is a form of sequencing. Taking a shower is not your highest priority for the morning—getting to the office is. But taking a shower is part of the sequence of events to get your highest priority accomplished.

Another wrinkle in the prioritization and sequencing discussion is that sequencing is not always optional. Let's go back to the example of getting to work. You have done your morning sequence with efficiency. Unfortunately, when you go to start your Tesla, you realize that the battery is running low. You will not have enough charge to get to the office. In an instant, your highest priority objective—getting to work—can't happen. It is blocked by an item in the longer sequence—charging your car.

Let's look at this same line of thinking in the world of software. A change to a team's application architecture needs to happen to support a strategic goal. A new set of database tables must get defined and implemented in the database structure. Architecture is not the priority; it is but a step in the sequence to achieve the final result.

This brings us to some information about dysfunctions in this area. Sequencing is often where office politics come to bear. Sequencing can get misinterpreted when the business side does not trust the technical side. In reality, prioritization is the steering wheel. Sequencing is the mechanics to translate intention into action. As change agents, we need to understand who is playing what roles and under what circumstances.

You Asked . . .

What if we find more work while we're doing the original work? Product development is, by nature, full of unknowns. Those unknowns become *knowns* through the learning that is done by the people doing the work. This work yields new items at all levels of the backlog. That can put any prioritized and sequenced plan at risk.

One common approach that teams use to decrease the risk involved in a body of work is the use of *spikes*. Spikes force learning to occur in a defined time box. That learning helps validate the approach that the team will likely use to solve a problem. It can also impact the list of priorities and the sequence of work.

Adding new work to a backlog, changing the list of priorities, changing the sequencing of work—none of these are indicators that you are *doing it wrong*. In fact, they are indicators that you are on the right track. If you were not doing any of these with some level of frequency— weekly or monthly (not daily)—then something is amiss because learning is not happening and feedback is not happening.

END-OF-CHAPTER QUESTIONS

Use the following to start a conversation about the contents of this chapter:

1. When planning work, do teams focus on priority or sequence? Both?
2. How often do priority and sequence match?

Section Two

Introspection

A WORK INTAKE CASE STUDY AS A BUSINESS NOVELLA, CHAPTER 2

The executives at Dandelion Software and Services expected more progress. The pace of progress on the new product is generating friction. Voices even got loud in the last management meeting.

Over the past several weeks, James has thought a lot about the difference between executive expectations and reality. Conversations with peers and stakeholders suggest organizational structure might be contributing to friction.

For the last several years, Dandelion has experienced explosive growth. However, more recently, key clients have had concerns about the architecture of the firm's flagship product and growth seems to be slowing. The private equity firms that have funded expansion are getting impatient. The organization's hierarchy and team structure has also grown. Most significant initiatives cut across several teams and departments. Outside of the executives, it's not clear which people influence the priority and order of work. Lack of transparency encourages people to use creative tactics to get work to the top of the queue. James listens to the conversations in the lunchroom and even in the brewpub down the street ("The Annex"). James concludes that work is overwhelming the teams. Priorities shift like everyone at a preschool soccer game. There's lots of running and changing directions. Everyone seems to have an opinion on who is in charge of the backlog. James decides it is time to facilitate another exercise to peel the work intake onion.

The organization's future depends on delivering the new product. James continues to focus on the organization that is most involved with the new product. It's the same cross-section of managers, team leads, and directors as the earlier workshop. James invites them to meet off-site. A few of the people aren't available, so James allows them to send trusted associates to take their place. Time and the market wait for no person.

James starts the workshop by providing context, then uses another version of the simplified organizational model, and recounts past conversations.

"It's not clear to me whose responsibility it is to determine who is doing what work, and when, for the new product." A lot of discussion follows. Nobody discounts the problem that lack of clarity is causing. The group then dives into the meat of the exercise.

James asks each participant to identify the people who play direct or influential roles in controlling work intake. By asking each person to complete a "People of Work Intake" worksheet on their own (see Figure S2.1), James avoids the immediate homogenization of group think. After working heads-down for 15 minutes, James facilitates a consolidation phase. While consolidating everyone's perceptions, the participants identify a core set of people. There was a mix of opinions about each person's involvement. The participants had a heated conversation which threatened the chance of coming to a consensus. To achieve a final consensus, James taped three forms to the wall. These forms described everyone that participants believed were part of work intake for the areas impacting the new product.

As the participants ate lunch, Anna, Dandelion's senior director who was most closely involved in the new product, gave voice to the elephant in the room. "This is messed up. No wonder we can't seem to get out of our own way. Everyone, including the janitor, has a hand in what gets done. And I don't mean that in a good way." With so many people involved in work intake, the strategic message was getting lost. Focus shifted from what was important to what was urgent.

After lunch, James led participants in the next few steps of their work intake discovery journey. James began by identifying the responsibilities of each person using the RAPIDS model:

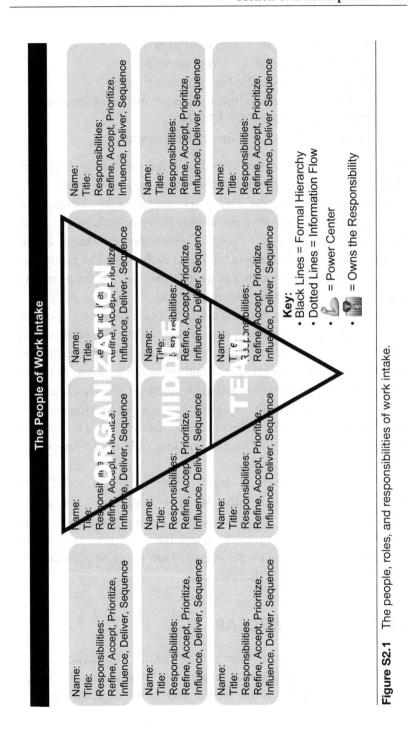

Figure S2.1   The people, roles, and responsibilities of work intake.

- **Refine:** Responsible for refining work
- **Accept:** Responsible for accepting work
- **Prioritize:** Responsible for prioritizing work
- **Influence:** Influences how work is prioritized or sequenced
- **Deliver:** Responsible for delivery
- **Sequence:** Responsible for sequencing work

The participants found that they had a mixture of agreement and disagreement around responsibilities. What was more troubling was that several people's responsibilities seemed to overlap. Three middle managers believed they were responsible for prioritization of the same work. "Well, that explains the politics," James thought. During a coffee break, James listened to people talking to each other. The participants were rationalizing the number of people involved and the overlaps in responsibilities. Anna was quiet and distant.

James decided not to push the group to a consensus on responsibilities. As a group, the workshop attendees completed an influence map. The attendees plotted the formal hierarchy on the model. Attendees then identified the important informal information flows. At the end of the exercise, it was obvious that work intake involved too many people. It was also obvious that information was not flowing well. One glaring surprise was that product management was out of the loop (see Figure S2.2). The informal information loops did not include middle management.

As James summarized the day's results, Anna interrupted, "I listened to a lot of discussion today. My knee-jerk reaction is to act. We can't wait much longer. Does anyone want to tell the board we can't get out of our own way? We need to determine if this mess is a problem soon. If we can't determine the impact, I am going to outsource this work." No one celebrated that evening.

EXECUTING NEW IDEAS

Now, it is your turn to consider who prioritizes and sequences work in the part of the organization you are most familiar with. If you have trouble conceptualizing a full vertical slice of the organization, never

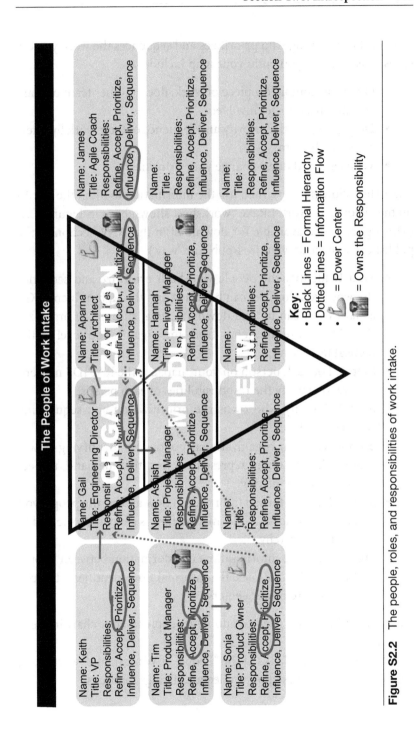

Figure S2.2   The people, roles, and responsibilities of work intake.

fear. Start by mapping who prioritizes and sequences the work you do. Questions to ask as you build your map include:

- Once you complete a piece of work, does another team or team member need to get involved?
- Do you impact the priority and sequence of their work by interacting with them?
- Who can (and does) change your priorities?

Study the following steps, then use the information to fill in the blanks on the "People of Work Intake" worksheet shown back in Figure S2.1. (This figure is also available for download in the WAV section of the publisher's website at www.jrosspub.com/wav.)

- **Step 1:** Identify the people who both prioritize and sequence the work you do. This can be direct and through influence. Go as far as you can up and down a vertical slice of the organization. Make sure it extends from the organization level to the tactical team level.
- **Step 2:** For each person on your map, use the RAPIDS nomenclature to identify the responsibilities of each person.
- **Step 3:** Identify who owns the prioritization and sequencing roles at each level.
- **Step 4:** Layer in organizational politics by identifying power centers. These often represent voices that demand respect during decision making.
- **Step 5:** Map the formal information flow among the people you identified. The formal information flow is generally expected to mirror the hierarchy.
- **Step 6:** Map the informal flow of information between people on the map. Many times, the informal flow identifies why specific people are power centers.

You may find that you need to add new people to your chart in Steps 5 and 6.

After filling in the blanks in the "People of Work Intake" worksheet, debrief on it with yourself or a colleague. Things to discuss:

- **Responsibilities**
  - ☐ How many people have more than one responsibility?
  - ☐ Are there overlaps in responsibilities?
  - ☐ Are responsibilities at the right level?
- **Ownership**
  - ☐ How challenging was it to identify who owns a responsibility?
- **Formal hierarchy and information flow**
  - ☐ Does the formal hierarchy match the flow of information? Why? Why not?
- **Power centers**
  - ☐ How challenging was it to identify the flow of information? How challenging was it to identify hierarchy and power centers?
  - ☐ Is power often centered in people who are higher in the formal hierarchy?
  - ☐ Does the informal information flow influence the power centers more than formal hierarchy?

What actions does your analysis suggest to make delivering value more consistent?

The following notes will help you to facilitate this exercise as a group event:

- Have each individual work on their own to identify who they think handles prioritization and sequencing. Then, work through consensus with the group.
- We often find that where the perceptions differ, the most actionable information is revealed. For example, we found that we had excluded someone who later became an important stakeholder. This is because, at first, we did not understand their influence on product architecture. Therefore, don't rush to consensus—discuss differences.

Section Three

Section Three

Work Intake Visualization: Metrics that Matter

Section Contents

SECTION INTRODUCTION

Measurement makes the process and impact of work intake explicit and visible. The goal of controlling work intake is to ensure the organization gets the right value when it is needed. This occurs by making sure organizations prioritize the right initiatives. Doing so allows teams to pull the right work when they have the capacity to get the work done. While that sounds simple, the real world is very complex. Measurement helps shine a spotlight on the work intake function. This enables improvement to happen. Having an opinion on whether that is happening does not always translate into action. Legendary management guru Peter Drucker said, "You can't improve what you don't measure." The current management trend is one of data-driven decision making. Most organizations somehow measure themselves. They might even measure the measures. Most of these measures and metrics are context-driven. They will not apply to every environment. We will not inventory all possible metrics and their corresponding permutations. Instead, we will focus on the one core area that matters across the board—*flow*.

16

FLOW

Flow is one of the most used words in agile and lean (and there are a lot of overused words in both fields). The word gets used by almost every practitioner every day. Yet, there are very few solid definitions. Most practitioners have a notional understanding of flow in software and software-related disciplines. They often revert to metaphors when challenged. If we had a dollar for every reference to a river or traffic, we would have been able to outbid Elon Musk for Twitter.

DEFINING FLOW

Flow can be used as a noun, a verb, or an adjective:

- As a noun: *a steady, continuous stream of something* (Oxford Languages)

- As a verb: *move along or out steadily and continuously in a current or stream* (Oxford Languages)
- As an adjective: *moving, proceeding, or shaped smoothly, gracefully, or continuously* (WordType.org)

In the context of product development, here are a few real-life examples of how we've heard people use the term *flow*:

- As a noun: *We are responsible for the flow of problem tickets from the call center.*
- As a verb: *Goals flow from the executives to middle management who craft initiatives.*
- As an adjective: *Flow efficiency is a great metric that is hard to measure for software teams.*

There are many more. Some are far less clear as to whether they fit any formal definition.

WHY A DEFINITION IS IMPORTANT

It is far easier to have a discussion after agreeing to a definition for an object or concept. For example, teams are a central component of all software-centric organizations. Work moves through teams, across teams, and between teams to finally get to done or canceled. Understanding the steps that a stream of work follows and the pace of the stream are important. Teams exist in every level of a company. The board of directors is as much a team as a software development team.

While writing this book, we searched for a definition of the word *flow* in a software context. We reviewed texts by Steve Tendon, David Anderson, Jim Benson, Mike Burrows, Matthew Skelton and Manual Pais, Capers Jones, and Tom Gilb. We found less than we expected.

The first solid definition was for personal flow, from the book *Flow*, by Mihaly Csikszentmihalyi. This form of flow, also known as being *in the zone*, reads:

"The state of being in which people become so immersed in the joy of their work or activity 'that nothing else seems to matter.'"[13]

Bill Burnett and Dave Evans advance this definition further in *Designing Your Life*, when they refer to flow as "engagement on steroids."[14] Both of these definitions are important; but they are not pertinent to flow in the context of software.

A definition that's more to the point for technical teams comes from Mik Kirsten's *Project to Product*:

"Software Flow: The activities involved in producing business value along a software value stream."[15]

Kersten's definition checks the box for the noun version of flow, but it misses on the critical component of movement. In the paragraph before the definition, he does reference work moving through the activities. Although we could infer movement, we want a more flexible definition of software flow.

Johanna Rothman pointed out that Daniel Vacanti defined flow in *Actionable Agile Metrics for Predictability*:

Flow is the movement and delivery of customer value through a process.[16]

---

[13] "Mihaly Csikszentmihalyi, pioneering psychologist and 'father of flow,' 1934–2021." University of Chicago News, 12/19/2022, news.uchicago.edu/story/mihaly-csikszent mihalyi-pioneering-psychologist-and-father-flow-1934-2021.

[14] Burnett, Bill and Evans, Dave. *Designing Your Life: How to Build a Well-Lived, Joyful Life*, Alfred A. Knopf, New York, NY, 2016. Audio Edition.

[15] Kersten, Mik. *Project to Product: How to Survive and Thrive in the Age of Digital Disruption with the Flow Framework*, IT Revolution Press, Portland, OR, 2018, p. 81. Kindle Edition.

[16] Vacanti, Daniel S. *Actionable Agile Metrics for Predictability: An Introduction*, ActionableAgile Press, 2018, p. 13. LeanPub Edition.

Rothman thinks this is a great definition, and we agree. It covers both the activities and movement of value. Given the fact that we now have a definition, let's turn our spotlight on the attributes used to describe flow.

FOUR COMMON ATTRIBUTES OF FLOW

Definitions provide a platform for establishing attributes to describe the object or idea. For example, if we were describing the flow of water, we could use direction, speed, and volume. Daniel Vacanti's definition of flow of software development and maintenance is, "the movement and delivery of customer value through a process." We can use this to identify a common set of attributes to describe flow. These attributes will be useful in the discussion of work intake. Attributes are critical because we need to communicate and measure nuances. If you only had one word to describe *rain* or *hot*, you'd miss a lot.

Different people have different thoughts on attributes of flow. Here's who we asked and what they said:

- **Scott Ambler,** author of *Disciplined Agile Delivery,* suggested "smoothness" and "scent." He added, "if the flow is turbulent or smells bad, there's likely an issue somewhere."
- **Mike Burrows,** author of *Kanban from the Inside,* responded with "smoothness, timeliness, good economic outcomes, and complexity."
- **Daniel Doiron,** author of *Tame Your Work Flow,* added "low flow load" (work in progress) and "slack."

These comments and other sources yield four high-level attributes of flow:

- **Capacity:** How many items can be in progress at any one time (not *in* the overall process, but actually being worked on—in progress)
- **Pace:** The speed at which work items move through the process or value chain

- **Variability:** The level of inconsistency inherent in the process
- **Value delivered:** The amount of benefit that ends up in end users' laps when it exits the process or value chain

Each of these attributes of flow is measurable. For example, flow velocity and throughput are measures of pace. Each attribute is also describable. This generates a cascade of attributes that better describe the concept and nuances. For example, we could use flow load (work in progress) to measure capacity. To better understand flow load, things such as touch time, status, slack, and open item aging are useful.

END-OF-CHAPTER QUESTIONS

Use the following to start a conversation about the contents of this chapter:

1. How is the word *flow* used in your workplace?
2. Describe a time where work was flowing well. Then, describe a time where work was not flowing well. What were the differences?
3. How does your team or organization track and use capacity, pace, variability, and value delivered?

17

FLOW METRICS

Learning Objectives—by the end of this chapter, you will be able to:
- ➤ Describe the basics of flow metrics
- ➤ Identify why measuring flow is important

INTRODUCTION

Measurement is an important tool to help teams and organizations ask the right questions. To borrow an idea from Daniel Vacanti's *Actionable Agile Metrics for Predictability*, measurement helps people ask the right questions sooner.

The way in which work enters any process has a major impact on what happens at the other end of the spectrum—delivery. Organizations and teams that can't control the amount and type of work that enters will incur the risk of overload. Too much work in progress foreshadows failure.

Getting the most value from a process is important to any leader. Yet, in today's dynamic environment, pure value maximization is rarely smart—other factors demand consideration. This makes selecting the right mix of metrics more difficult. For example, balancing the *most value* with *getting value sooner* complicates the discussion. In some cases, getting some value sooner is worth more than the same value delivered later. Guiding the delivery of value is complicated. It's more than ordering a backlog and hoping for execution efficacy and efficiency.

We measure in order to ask the right questions. Flow metrics provide input and feedback into the process of managing the flow of value. Metrics alone rarely suffice. We still need a mind (or minds) to weigh context before making decisions. Flow metrics provide a powerful set of tools to generate information about the flow of value. After all, delivering value is the only reason software teams exist.

You Asked . . .

Are you going to talk about how to use story points? We've worked with organizations and teams who have used story-point estimation. Our mileage has varied. Some firms understand the premise of story points. They are a proxy for a discussion around size and complexity of a work item. They are also a tool to avoid the toxic discussion of effort hours. Others get hung up on story-point estimation being an exact science. They seek mastery for fear of consequences.

Both camps seem to have drifted away from two fundamental concepts:

- Focusing on the value of the work (both to customers and the company)
- How the work actually gets done (i.e., flow)

We have seen much more substantive change occur when firms can see how work is getting done. They do this using flow metrics instead of haggling over whether a story is two or three points.

FLOW METRICS BASICS

Before we dive into flow metrics, there are a few basic concepts to discuss and understand.

Flow Items: The Basis for Flow Metrics

Every organization defines and names the containers that become work items. The things that teams call their work reflect personal style and culture. This makes any macro discussion of flow metrics problematic without a framework. Mik Kersten, in *Project to Product*, defines a *flow item* as:

> *A unit of business value pulled by a stakeholder through a product's value stream.*[17]

Kersten goes on further and groups flow items into four categories,[18] as shown in Table 17.1.

To get an understanding of the prevalent flow items in your context, we recommend:

1. Mapping the whole value stream
2. Taking inventory of all flow items across the value stream
3. Mapping each flow item to one of the four categories

When categorizing flow items, ensure that each item belongs to one (and only one) category. Each item has a *mutually exclusive and collectively exhaustive* category (MECE). In cases where a flow item spawns more items, categorize the parent item. For example, a story requires the completion of four tasks and three subtasks. In this example, measure the story as a single flow item since it is the container. Do not count all seven of the tasks and subtasks as discrete pieces of work.

---

[17] Kersten, Mik. *Project to Product: How to Survive and Thrive in the Age of Digital Disruption with the Flow Framework*, IT Revolution Press, Portland, OR, 2018, p. 84. Kindle Edition.

[18] Synthesized from *Project to Product: How to Survive and Thrive in the Age of Digital Disruption with the Flow Framework*.

Table 17.1   Flow Item Categories

Category	Definition	Flow Item Examples
Features	Items that deliver business value	• Epics • User stories • Requirements
Defects	Items that, when completed, deliver quality	• Bugs • Defects • Anomalies • *Opportunities* (when you aren't allowed to use the word *defect*)
Risks	Items for security, governance, and compliance	• Findings • Vulnerabilities • Regulatory items
Debts	Items that remove impediments to future delivery	• Refactoring • Infrastructure automation

---

You Asked . . .

What is a MECE?

MECE is a categorization approach introduced by Barbara Minto of McKinsey & Company. The approach arranges and categorizes items, so that any one item belongs in one—and only one—category. This reduces the possibility of double-counting observations. It also reduces the possibility of arguing over gray areas.

An example of a MECE would be grouping people by what year they were born. Everyone has one—and only one—birth year. Nobody can be born in two different years. On the other hand, an example of a non-MECE category would be classifying people by eye color. Some people may have eyes of different colors or (unfortunately) have no eyes.

Flow Load: Work in Action (Hopefully)

Flow load is the amount of work that you have begun but has not yet exited the system. This is regardless of whether the item is active or delayed. One of the basic assumptions of flow load—and flow metrics—is that work arrives, gets completed, and then departs. Value comes when the work leaves the process. Keeping an eye on flow load is an excellent way to observe and predict system performance. For example, as more work starts and does not finish, flow load increases. System performance falls due to this churn. This leads to less work (and value) delivered.

To determine flow load, count the discrete units of customer value that have entered the process but have not exited. There is no acknowledgment of size or complexity.

You Asked . . .

Is work that somebody added to my backlog considered to be flow load? Or, when does work become flow load? The simple answer is that if you have not pulled the item to begin work, it is not flow load. Defining when work arrives, though, is often harder than defining when it is complete. Daniel Vacanti, author of *Actionable Agile Metrics for Predictability*, points out that the definition of *arrival* is easier in a pull system than it is in a push system.

In pull systems, work gets pulled from the backlog when capacity is available. Work arrives when the team pulls it from the backlog.

In push systems, work gets assigned. Determining when an item *arrives* is harder to define. To wit—does shoving work into someone's queue mean that it has started? Defect triage is one example. We have worked in environments where a team (or teams) triage defects for a period of time. In this scenario, a team immediately inspects incoming problems to determine their severity. If the problem meets certain criteria, the team invests more time in the item. They may determine (and perform) the fix. They may also assign a separate team to fix it. If the defect doesn't meet those criteria, the team will close the problem or move it to the backlog. This is an example of pushing work to a team, so arrival was easy to determine. Flow load varies based on the severity of the problem and whether the team works on items past the triage step.

Teams in push systems typically have higher flow load than those in pull systems. This is because saying "yes" to work is easier than telling people that work will need to wait until later. There is less (or zero) consideration of team capacity in push systems than in pull systems. This is a basis for overload.

Lead Time

David J. Anderson defines *lead time* in the Kanban Maturity Model as, "starting at the mutually agreed commitment point and continuing until an item is ready for delivery." In other words, lead time is the time between when we agree to do a piece of work until delivery.

A critical decision in calculating lead time is the point when the clock starts ticking. If the act of putting something on the backlog is a commitment to perform, then lead time starts at that point. (We don't think that putting something on a backlog is a commitment. We recommend emptying and replenishing backlogs with some frequency.) While lead time is important to customers, it is rarely used in flow metrics.

Flow Time (Cycle Time)

Flow time—aka cycle time—is the amount of elapsed time that a work item spends as work in process. Flow time is a direct reflection of the calendar. The calendar is the one element every customer understands. Flow time includes all calendar time between starting and completing. This includes any delays that may manifest themselves.

Flow time is useful for answering the second most popular question in software development, "When will it be done?" Flow time is also a good proxy for predicting cost. The longer a piece of work takes to complete, the more costly it will be. This is because labor is often the largest cost in the world of software development.

Flow Time/Lead Time Relationship

We have heard these terms used as synonyms. They're similar concepts and often confused. When working with these terms, ensure that you have a common understanding of both. They are not the same, but they are related. *Lead time* is the full duration—how long it takes from imagining the work (put on the backlog) to delivery. *Flow time* is the amount of time it takes from start to finish. Flow time is a subset of lead time; it will always be less.

You Asked . . .

How do I measure flow time if my company batches up work items for deployment/release? We have worked with many different types of teams during our careers. The majority of those teams do not deliver stories directly to customers. Instead, the teams complete work and promote their changes to the main line of the code base. At some point, the business makes a decision that it's time to release a new version. Whatever code is part of the main line of the code base at that point becomes released.

In contexts like these, measuring flow time provides only a partial picture. As an alternative, consider *start* and *deliver* as parts of the development process. Flow time can measure the time it takes from the team starting the work to the team finishing the work.

Touch Time

Touch time is the amount of time spent working on the item. It is measured while the item is in progress. Touch time owes a debt to manufacturing; it is literally the time spent touching the work. Touch time is the opposite of a delay, which is the time an item is inactive, waiting, or on hold. An example of a delay is a piece of partially done work that is waiting for a meeting which no one can make until next week.

Flow Efficiency

- Flow efficiency is the ratio of touch time to lead time[19]
- Flow efficiency percent = touch time ÷ lead time × 100
- Any reduction in the amount of delay improves overall flow efficiency

---

[19] If you want to understand how work flows through the system after it starts, calculate flow efficiency using cycle time instead of lead time. Calculating flow efficiency using lead time is often desirable, though. It provides a vivid picture of how long stakeholders wait for promises to get delivered.

BASIC METRICS OF FLOW

Flow metrics are most valuable in measuring value streams (see Table 17.2). They are also used as a tool to measure team health and the impact of changes to work intake practices and policies.

Table 17.2 Basic Flow Metrics

Metric	Definition	Equation	For Example
Flow Time (Cycle Time)	How long it takes for an item to move from started to delivered. When measuring a value stream, use the lead time for the entire value stream. When measuring a team, use the time an item gets pulled from the backlog to the time it reaches production.	Release date *minus* acceptance date	An item is started on Monday and delivered on Friday. The flow time for this item is four days.
Flow Items Distribution	How many work items (by type) are completed per period.	Each of the following shows as a percentage of the total: • Sum of feature flow items completed • Sum of risk flow items completed • Sum of defect flow items completed • Sum of debt items completed	A team completed 10 defects and 20 stories in a 30-day period. The flow distribution for this 30-day period is 67% features and 33% defects.

Table 17.2 *continued*

Metric	Definition	Equation	For Example
Flow Load (Work in Progress)	The amount of flow load in the process being measured.	Sum of all work items in progress	A team has 10 items in progress on the 5th day of the sprint. Their flow load is 10 items.
Flow Efficiency	How much time work items are being worked on, compared to the total time work items are in the process. Analogous to *takt time* in manufacturing.	Total touch time (time actually working on an item) ÷ total time in progress	An item spent four business days in progress, but was only being worked on for 20 minutes. The flow efficiency for this item is 20 ÷ 5,760 = 0.34%.
Flow Velocity (Throughput)	How many work items move through the process per unit of time.	Total number of work items completed in a period	A team completed 15 items during the first week of February. The flow velocity for this time period is 15.

Experience Report

Flow Time—Not Just from Start to Finish

Flow time quantifies the time it takes work to get from *in progress* to *done*. But what about measuring flow time in a more granular fashion? When Jeremy began working with a Scrum team, he started collecting flow time data. He used this data during a sprint retrospective.

continued

As the team reflected on their flow time, a team member wondered how long it was taking to deliver their changes; it was a great question. The team was coming off a sprint that had been littered with continuous integration/continuous delivery (CI/CD) problems, which delayed the final step—delivery. Another team was already working to resolve those CI/CD challenges, but the question about how long it took to deliver changes got Jeremy to start tracking flow time in each phase. The phases matched the columns on the team's Kanban board—investigation, code, test, review, and deliver. Tracking flow time in this granular fashion was a bit more manual than Jeremy would have liked. Yet, collecting this data led to a valuable retrospective. The team committed themselves to reducing time in review, which reduced the overall flow time.

Flow Velocity

Flow velocity (throughput) is a measure of the number of items that enter and exit the process in a given period. Observing the departure rate is the way to measure flow velocity. The departure rate shows how many work items are completed and exit the process in a given period. Arrival rate, which should be the mirror image of departure rate, can also be an important metric. If arrival rate exceeds departure rate, flow load and flow time will increase.

Escape Rate

Another metric that can be very helpful in contexts where teams are planning on cadence (iterating) is *escape rate*. Escape rate is the proportion of work planned in a period but not finished. One example is stories. To calculate escape rate for stories, take the *number of committed stories not completed* and divide by the *total number of committed stories*. For example, a team planned 10 stories in a sprint, but only finished 5. The escape rate is $5 \div 10 = 50\%$.

END-OF-CHAPTER QUESTIONS

Use the following to start a conversation about the contents of this chapter:

1. How many of the basic metrics of flow are your team or organization already surfacing?
2. How does your team and organization manage flow?
3. Where could your team or organization expand its use of flow metrics?

18

FLOW METRICS PALETTE

Learning Objectives—by the end of this chapter, you will be able to:
> ‣ Describe what comprises a palette of flow metrics

Flow metrics give process transparency to organizations that use continuous flow models (kanban). They also play well with Scrum (or Scrumban). Each flow metric follows work entering and exiting a system. They conform to the basic requirements for measurement to be valuable:

- Accuracy
- Precision (at the right level)
- Repeatability
- Understanding (a shared understanding of what is being measured)

How data gets used and collected has affected this flow metrics palette. For example, a previous iteration of our flow metrics palette included velocity. Velocity is often calculated using story points; and the concept of story points is often abused. For this reason, we thought it was dangerous (or at best, valueless) to look at velocity in order to understand flow. We also thought about contexts like contracts and pricing, where productivity and estimation are important metrics. Here, using the International Function Point Users Group function points will prove more valuable than velocity (story points). Story points can be useful at a team level as a tool to control work intake. We've found that understanding throughput generally yields better conversations and outcomes.

Different measures and metrics are useful in different situations. All metrics describe a moment in time. Trends of specific metrics describe change over time. Other metrics are useful in predicting the future. The following automobile analogy is useful to illustrate the point: the dashboard tells the driver what is happening to the car in the present, while the rearview mirror shows the driver what is happening behind the car. The following sections continue embellishing our flow-metrics-as-automobile-features analogy.

DASHBOARD METRICS

Dashboard metrics show what is currently happening in the team or organization. These metrics will change based on current decisions. The following subsections present examples of dashboard metrics.

Flow Load (Work in Progress or WIP)

Flow load is the amount of work that has entered the process but has not exited. It is synonymous with WIP. Flow load even includes the stuff you have put on hold. Whether it's because you're waiting until another team is ready or waiting for someone to come back from medical leave. Work that starts but is not done or canceled is considered to be in progress. It is flow load. Flow load places cognitive load on teams, value streams, and organizations.

Flow load indicates over/underutilization of teams, value streams, and organizations. Too much or too little flow reduces efficiency and effectiveness. When work intake is not under control, the amount of work that is in process will either build up or slow to a trickle. It's feast or famine. The load on the system reduces the ability to deliver quality output.

The visualization in Figure 18.1 uses the concept of flow items from Dr. Mik Kersten's book *Project to Product*. In the example, there are 20 items in process. The flow load, then, is 20. The six done items are not used in calculating flow load.

Any specific flow load number is neither good nor bad. Flow load provides information about present performance of a team or value stream. It can also help predict future performance. Surfacing flow load data enables conversations about flow load limits. Flow load limits are a desirable outcome of those conversations. This flow load limit represents the line where efficacy begins to decline. Exceeding this line for any length of time is detrimental. Exceeding the flow load limit is the single largest predictor of flow velocity and flow time; doing so reduces flow velocity and elongates flow time.

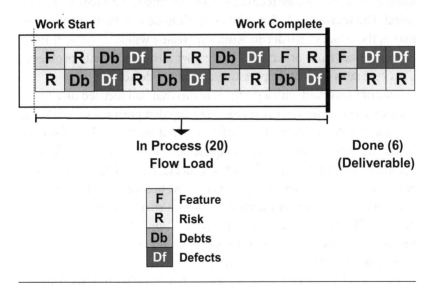

Figure 18.1   An example of flow load.

Flow Distribution

Flow distribution is the amount of work and types of work that a process or team has in process at any given time. It is represented as the ratio of each flow item or work type within a system and/or value stream. Flow distribution is useful for providing context for the other flow metrics. It serves two forward-looking purposes:

1. At a macro level, flow distribution helps the organization to understand whether work is in sync with strategic goals. It helps understand the distribution of features, risks, defects, and debt. This data is an input into whether the organization is progressing toward future revenue and growth.
2. At a tactical level, flow distribution indicates whether one type of work is being prioritized over others. This data is useful for organizations and teams.

Let's look at an example of flow distribution in action. Teams that favor feature work and ignore technical debt will find themselves in a death spiral. The increasing technical debt leads to defects in the product, or makes the product harder to work on. Teams will have to shift more capacity away from other work to deal with the immediate problems. This generates even more pressure, and often, defects.

One of us worked with a group of teams that had focused on a large-scale conversion for over two years. During that period, any work that did not threaten human life or safety was put on the backlog for later. When the conversions were complete, the teams had a backlog of several thousand items. This included debts, risks, defects, and small enhancements. The set of applications had become a horror story to work on. Two years after the conversions finished, the teams still had a backlog. The pain of working on the applications also caused employee turnover. The moral of this story is that what you work on has an impact today, as well as into the future.

Figures 18.2 and 18.3 show a couple of approaches to visualize flow distribution. Flow distribution is most effective when work is consistently categorized and collected. We recently worked with a Scrum

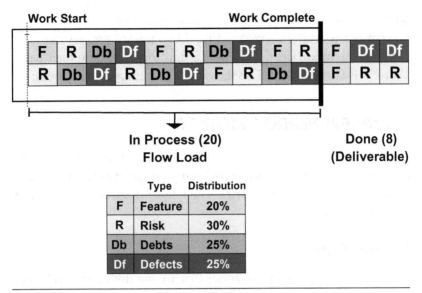

Figure 18.2   An example of flow distribution.

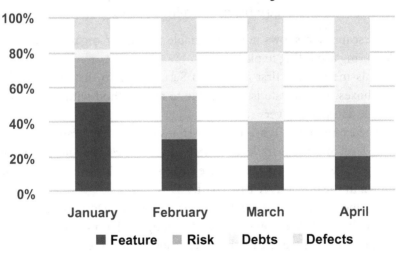

Figure 18.3   Another example of flow distribution.

team that had a working agreement with their product owner. Fifteen percent of the work in any sprint would go toward process improvement and technical debt. They have a flow load graph on their dashboard. It is always updated, so their work allocation is transparent.

REARVIEW MIRROR METRICS

Rearview mirror metrics reflect performance in the recent past and also trends across time. Changes to teams or organizations take time to show an impact on these metrics. The following subsections describe examples of these metrics.

Escape Rate

Escape rate is the number of stories that are not done (deployable) by the end of a timebox. This timebox can be a sprint (Scrum or Scrumban) or predicted timebox (kanban). You can calculate escape rate using the following formula:

$$\text{quantity of committed stories not completed} \div$$
$$\text{quantity of committed stories}$$

The escape rate shows how predictable a team or organization is at delivering according to plan.

This metric was first applied to Scrum, due to that framework's timeboxes. Escape rate is extendable to any method with timeboxes, release dates, or delivery dates.

The example in Figure 18.4 illustrates using escape rate at the release level and the team level. A second view of escape rate, as shown in Figure 18.5, displays the last five sprints, including the three sprints shown in the previous release chart.

Escape rate is a great metric to chart and trend. Doing so gives you data to have a discussion regarding breaking work down and/or biting off more than a team can chew. Retrospectives are great venues for

Release-Level Escape Rate

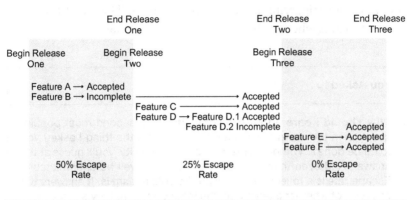

Figure 18.4   An example of release-level escape rate.

Escape Rate for Last Five Sprints

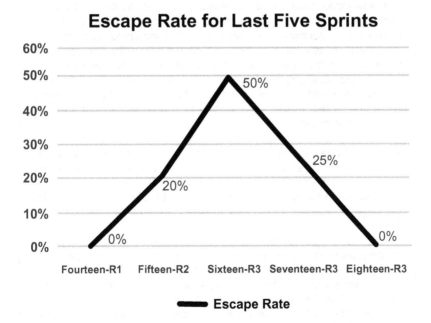

Figure 18.5   An example of sprint-level escape rate.

these discussions to take place. Dramatic changes and upward trends are useful for triggering targeted retrospectives. The trend over time also tells teams whether they are becoming predictable.

You Asked . . .

Why should I care about predictability? The second most popular question in the world of software is, "When will the thing I asked you to do be done?" Without some level of predictability, you'll guess at the answer. And even then, that answer may very well be unpredictable. Escape rate is a reflection of how predictable a team is. It answers the question of whether a team gets the thing done that they say they will. Scaled Agile Framework® 6.0 includes a release train predictability metric that resembles escape rate. Expressing predictability is more than spin.

We've worked with teams that seem to have solved the predictability challenge. They've done so by doing some of the basics. They base plans on past performance. They say "no" to incoming work and they work together as a team to get work finished before the iteration ends. We've always found that these teams are happy and satisfied much more so than teams without control over work intake—even if the work they're doing isn't the most absorbing. They've found the "sustainable pace" mentioned in the Agile Manifesto. It's some form of software development nirvana.

The flip side of the coin includes the teams we have worked with that have gamed the predictability metric. They under plan on purpose. They nudge up their estimates of stories to look like they're getting more done, and they rarely take any chances. They end iterations with predictability measures that always land at 100 percent or above. Yet, the larger goals—feature delivery, releases, etc.—rarely seem on track. These are antipatterns.

One last thing on escape rate—it's important to note that this metric is about committed stories at the start of an iteration. "We were going to get these 10 stories done in this iteration. How many of the 10 stories did we get done?" We have worked with teams and programs that define predictability as the number of stories completed in the iteration, regardless of whether those stories were part of the plan. We have seen examples where a team plans 10 stories, revises the plan on day three of the sprint, and gets 10 completely different stories completed. Is that true predictability? No. Was it the right business decision? That is a different conversation.

Flow Time (Cycle Time)

Flow time (cycle time) measures how long it takes teams to complete work. It starts when an item goes in the backlog and ends when it's released. Understanding flow time helps teams and organizations understand how predictable they are.

Figure 18.6 shows an example of a common pattern for completion of work items.

As you can infer from the previous figure, the time an item takes from start to completion varies. Even if some of the aforementioned steps happen quickly, software is not building widgets. In software development, performance rarely follows a normal curve. Analyzing flow time requires developing an understanding of the variability in duration of items.

The scatter plot diagram shown in Figure 18.7 illustrates this type of variability. This example illustrates a common pattern of performance. Half of the items complete in 10 days or less, while others take much longer. To get more insight into the data, use percentiles and the median (the 50th percentile). For flow time, half the observations occur below the median and half above.

After collecting flow time data, identify the median and the 85th percentile. Knowing both provides a tool to forecast when a work item will finish. In the illustrated example, let's say the median is five days,

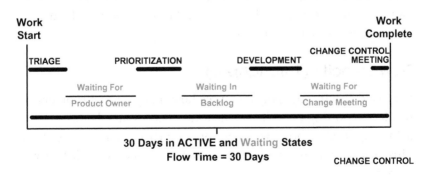

Figure 18.6 A common pattern for completion of work items.

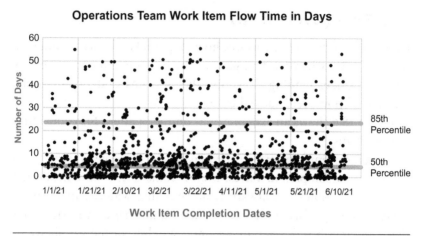

Figure 18.7   A scatter plot of work item completion.

and the 85th percentile is 30 days. The team can say with confidence that they can complete most work items within 30 days or less. In software development, being able to forecast with confidence is a powerful thing.

Comparing the 85th percentile to the median is also a good indicator of variability. The higher the ratio between the 85th percentile and the median, the more variability. In that example, if the 85th percentile is 30 days and the median is five days, then the ratio is 6:1. For a frame of reference, 2:1 is a solid level of variability for a team doing a mix of development and support. Variability occurs because of many factors, most of which are controllable. Use tools like retrospectives to identify experiments to control variation.

Flow Velocity (Throughput)

Flow velocity (throughput) measures how many items customers get within a reporting period. This measure focuses on whether you are delivering. It also shows whether you are delivering more over time. This measure ties to the principles in the Manifesto for Agile Software Development:

- "Working software is the primary measure of progress"

- "Deliver working software frequently, from a couple of weeks to a couple of months, with a preference to the shorter timescale"

Figures 18.8 and 18.9 each exhibit an example that shows an approach to visualize flow velocity.

Teams can use median flow velocity data over longer periods for release planning. Flow velocity provides a basis for answering when a

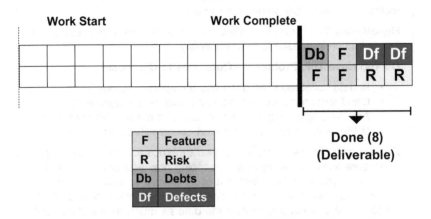

Figure 18.8   An example of flow velocity.

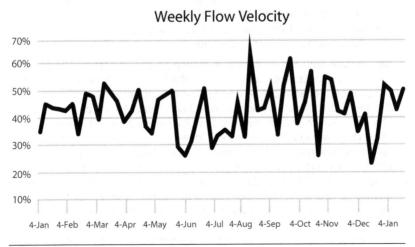

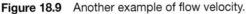

Figure 18.9   Another example of flow velocity.

group of work items will finish. If a team is pursuing process improvement, it's expected that flow velocity will improve.

Experiment

Problem: Metrics are only as good as the data behind them. When data behind metrics are questionable, people question the usefulness of the metric. The metric becomes meaningless.

Hypothesis: When people understand data collection for metrics, the metric has an increased level of credibility.

Do You Have This Problem?—Questions to Diagnose.
- Is data collected in an open and transparent manner?
- Can team members see the same data as management?
- Are there agreed upon ways to calculate metrics across teams?
- Is the process for collecting data documented and visible?

Experiment: The next time you present metrics to a group of people, make sure to spend some time describing how you got the data. For example, if you're pulling data out of an electronic tool, describe the query or function you used. Give the group a chance to inspect the process that you used to collect the data as much as the data itself. Document the process and the feedback so that anyone can refer to it.

Validation: Validation ensures a common understanding of the data collection process. You might have to describe the process for collecting data a few times for it to sink in. Whenever data fidelity is being questioned, remind the audience of the process. Refer them to whatever documentation exists to describe the data collection process.

Example: A new Scrum Master is joining an existing team. The previous Scrum Master took a new role in the firm and spent a few hours handing off the team before exiting. The next sprint review is soon and the new Scrum Master needs to collect some data for the conversation. The new Scrum Master reviews the old Scrum Master's documents. They discover that they were not pulling flow time data out of the electronic ticketing tool. The new Scrum Master has done this with other teams and proceeds to gather this data in the exact same way. When showing flow time data during the sprint review, a team member speaks up and says, "This can't be right. There's no way it takes us that long to close stories." After the sprint review, the Scrum Master shows the team how they collected flow time data. The team uses the sprint retrospective to discuss flow time. The team creates two improvement items for the next sprint.

END-OF-CHAPTER QUESTIONS

Use the following to start a conversation about the contents of this chapter:

1. How would you collect the dashboard metrics described in this chapter?
2. How would you use the dashboard metrics described in this chapter?
3. How would you collect the rearview mirror metrics described in this chapter?
4. How would you use the rearview mirror metrics described in this chapter?

19

FLOW METRICS AT
ALL LEVELS

Learning Objectives—by the end of this chapter, you will be
able to:
- ➤ Describe the goals of each level in the organizational hierarchy
- ➤ Describe the use of flow metrics at all three levels—organization, middle, and team

The flow metrics that we have already discussed focused on different aspects of a value chain. Combine the metrics to get different views—for example, organizational data, product or value chain data, or team-level data. While robust, flow metrics are not the only set of measures that an organization needs. They are a great place to begin after satisfying basic legal requirements. For example, almost every firm needs financial measures (budgets and profit margins). A focus on flow provides powerful intelligence to teams, middle management, and executives. Different flow metrics are applicable to different levels in a company's hierarchy.

Figure 19.1 demonstrates an overview of the big picture, which we will unpack in further sections.

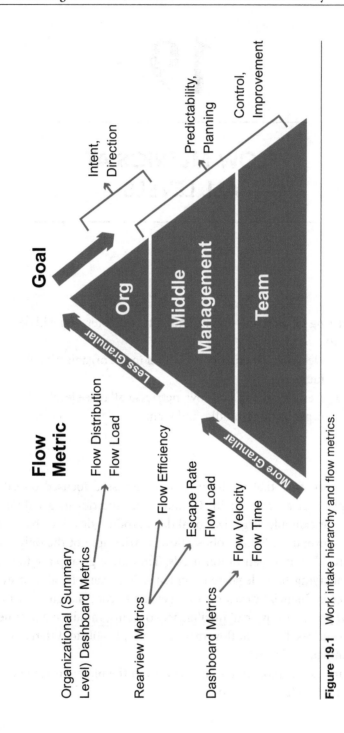

Figure 19.1 Work intake hierarchy and flow metrics.

ORGANIZATION

The organization level is the strategic part of the hierarchy. This level establishes the vision, mission, and goals of the entire organization. It controls budgets, money, people, and resources at a macro level. The organization level formulates intent. Executives decide on direction, and how to deploy people and resources. For example, executives at this level establish the budget for software development. They do not decide who gets hired as a junior programmer.

We recommend using the flow metrics that are shown in Table 19.1 at the organization level.

Table 19.1   Recommended Organizational-Level Flow Metrics

Metric	Why?	Type
Flow Distribution	Provides a visualization of strategy. How do we want to deploy our people? Gives executives an understanding of compliance toward goals for types of work.	Dashboard
Flow Load	Tells leaders whether their organization is absorbing more WIP (work in progress) than can flow. While flow load can provide real-time feedback, it is generally reviewed on a periodic basis. This makes it a rearview mirror metric, providing more of a *where we were* view than a *where we are* view.	Rearview mirror

MIDDLE MANAGEMENT

Middle management occupies the level between the executives and the teams. This level translates the strategic goals of executives into tactical plans. It includes features and epics. Those tactical plans are then translated into something more actionable (work items). Middle management's goals are predictability and planning. Both build trust.

Those in the middle have to navigate pressure from stakeholders. These stakeholders do not have direct influence over goals or initiatives. Professional biases impact flow distribution in the middle. So does pressure from stakeholders to deliver specific work.

We recommend using the flow metrics shown in Table 19.2 in the middle level.

Table 19.2 Recommended Middle-Level Flow Metrics

Metric	Why?	Type
Flow Distribution	This metric shows how the organization is using its capacity, as reflected in the type of work items it is delivering.	Dashboard
Flow Load	Delivers information about what is being worked on today. This can be across teams or aggregated at the value chain or department. While often viewed on a periodic basis, middle management can vary flow load in the short term to achieve specific goals.	Rearview mirror
Flow Efficiency	Delivers information on the amount of delay that is occurring in the flow of work.	Rearview mirror
Flow Velocity	Delivers information on the amount of work that is being delivered per period. Flow velocity is only known after work finishes, which is a rearview mirror metric. Use historical data to calculate the median and 85th percentile flow velocity.	Rearview mirror

TEAM

Teams process priorities from a wide variety of stakeholders. They then generate a sequence for doing the work. At the team level, sequencing—what has to go first, second, third, etc.—is a technical discussion.

We recommend using the flow metrics shown in Table 19.3 at the team level.

Table 19.3   Recommended Team-Level Flow Metrics

Metric	Why?	Type
Flow Time	Flow time reflects how long work items are in process. Time is a reflection of: • The health of the process • Understanding the work • Work decomposition • The presence of bottlenecks Use flow time to adjust priorities based on local context. At a team level, flow time provides information so the team can adjust.	Dashboard
Flow Velocity	Flow velocity shows how much work is delivered per period, which allows teams to field questions about when work will be completed. This can be used to adjust priorities based on local context. At a team level, this metric provides information so that the team can adjust what they are doing today and tomorrow.	Rearview mirror
Flow Load (WIP)	For teams, flow load shows how much work the team has started that is still on their proverbial plate. Teams can watch this on a real-time basis then react to it.	Dashboard
Flow Efficiency	For teams, flow efficiency shows how much time gets spent working on work items. It also shows how much time they spend sitting around. This metric is a clear process improvement tool.	Rearview mirror
Escape Rate	Committed vs. completed at the end of the timebox. Used to improve planning. A high escape rate correlates to low trust in team performance.	Rearview mirror

END-OF-CHAPTER QUESTIONS

Use the following to start a conversation about the contents of this chapter:

1. What flow information are the leaders of your organization interested in? How is that communicated?
2. When was the last time that flow metrics were part of the department meeting?
3. How does (or would) the teams in your company use flow metrics?

20

METRICS ANTIPATTERNS

Learning Objectives—by the end of this chapter, you will be able to:
- ▸ Describe antipatterns related to metrics
- ▸ Describe how to resolve metrics antipatterns

There are an endless array of things to measure in the world of software development. Some of them are useful; others, not so much. In this section, we are going to examine metrics antipatterns we have seen over the course of our careers.

STORY POINTS (AS THROUGHPUT AND/OR VELOCITY MEASURES)

Story points are a very popular tool for agile teams and organizations. Their use is not part of the Scrum Guide (and never has been). Still, it has become the most common way that Scrum teams estimate work and calculate progress. When done well, it is a step forward from some of the old ways of estimating software—"How many hours is that going to take?"

Use of story points is not, in and of itself, an antipattern. But what your team or organization is doing with them might very well be. Many story point antipatterns are due to the confusion over what story points are and how to use them. Here are some examples:

- Are story points meant to mean size?
- Are story points meant to include complexity?
- What numeric scale gets used to size items with story points?
- Who should actually size stories?
- Are story points unique to teams, or can you use them to compare performance across teams?
- Are story points relative?
- Or—the king of them all—can you equate story points with hours?

The answers to these questions can vary. It depends on the person or body of knowledge you are consulting.

We have worked in contexts where story points were useful. We have also worked in contexts where they were useless (or worse). Let's expand on those thoughts.

Here's where we have seen story points prove useful:

- When teams use them to promote conversations about prioritization of value delivery
- When teams spend more time talking about acceptance criteria than whether the item is two or three points
- When teams have the autonomy to estimate work on their own, all together, as a whole team
- Where teams have enough run time together that they have a solid set of historical data; this data helps with forecasting
- Where teams don't conflate story points and effort

Here's where we've seen story points drifting into antipattern territory:

- When teams and organizations focus on getting good at the act of estimation. ("We estimated this story as a three, but it took an entire sprint to complete. Let's do a targeted retrospective on this topic!")

- When story points become a proxy measure for hours. ("It's going to take a day to do that, so it must be one point.")
- When one person on the team—for example, the team lead—decides on the number of points for product backlog items. ("The team lead estimated the entire product backlog in preparation for sprint planning.")
- When someone who is not on the team estimates the work. ("The architect in our area estimated our entire backlog of work.")

Story points are not an easy concept for everyone to grasp; but they are also not rocket science. If you find that your team or organization's use of story points is starting to smell like an antipattern, try these antidotes:

- Find a body of knowledge that explains the concept in a consistent, reasonable fashion. Get everyone to read it and agree to those rules. This should help reset whatever ambiguity exists around the topic of story points. If you're going to use story points, we recommend referring to Mike Cohn's writing on the topic.[20]
- Build up a body of data using the flow metrics we have discussed, and shift the team and/or organization to focus more on those measures than anything related to story points. (A common pattern that we've seen in our careers is that teams and organizations start with story points and then transition to the flow metrics.)

MEASURING INDIVIDUALS

In the world of software development, teams are the proverbial atomic unit. Organizations group their people in teams to deliver value. They

---

[20] "What Are Agile Story Points?" Mountain Goat Software, 2/14/2023, www.mountaingoatsoftware.com/blog/what-are-story-points.

do this because a group of people can deliver value faster than a single person working 80 hours per week. But how are individuals within a team measured? Here are four classic organizational antipatterns for measuring individuals:

- How many tickets did a person complete over a period of time?
- How many lines of code did a person deliver over a period of time? (A variant is counting the number of commits.)
- How many defects did a person introduce to the code base over a period of time?
- How many hours did a person log or bill over a period of time? (A variant is counting the number of keystrokes from the corporate key logging software.)

These antipatterns focus on individuals over the outcomes delivered by a team.

Why do organizations need to measure performance of individuals rather than teams? The majority of organizations still function under a yearly performance review paradigm. Performance impacts compensation and promotion. People managers want performance data to justify their compensation and promotion decisions. Modern engineering tools make it easy to look at performance data. This could include completed tickets, lines of code, and defects fixed (or generated). Reviewing this data can also happen well after the fact. Alas, it will be long after the context behind why the numbers were what they were is lost. Regardless of the lack of context, the numbers are defensible.

In our experience, measuring teams rather than individuals delivers more value. Measuring teams promotes people working together to achieve a goal. In many teams, the contributions of each person might not be evident by looking at a team's board. A report of what happened over the past few weeks might not show this either. How many lines of code can you attribute to someone who is desk-checking a colleague's test cases? We've worked with teams where members contributed to the success of the team by pair programming, reviewing code and providing feedback, or even running interference on things like defect triage. The outcomes a team delivers are more important than the number of code commits from all the individuals combined.

If you find that the previously listed antipatterns are present in your context, try these antidotes:

- Coach middle managers that evaluating people involves more than looking at an electronic ticketing system. It involves things like:
  - Observing the team operating for a period of time (akin to a Gemba walk)
  - Surveying other team members to understand how each person works with peers
  - Evaluating the outcomes that the team delivers
- Ask middle managers what team and individual performance data matters most to them because you want alignment between both data points
- Be willing to offer feedback to managers on specific individuals, and if you're going to collect data on specific people, make sure it comes with the context behind the data

TEAM VERSUS TEAM

Not all teams are created equal. If you'll allow a baseball analogy, not all baseball teams are the 1927 New York Yankees. There was only one of those teams. That team featured Lou Gehrig and Babe Ruth. Even the 1928 New York Yankees were not the same as the 1927 New York Yankees. And not all software development teams feature the equivalent of Gehrig and Ruth. But that's okay.

This antipattern occurs when someone uses a measure or metric to compare teams to each other. A popular data point to use for this comparison is story point velocity. "Why can Team A get 50 story points done in an iteration, but Team B only gets 25 done? They have the same number of people on the team. Team A must be top performers." This antipattern builds upon measuring each individual's antipatterns, then extrapolating them to the entire team.

Comparing teams with most metrics isn't useful for the following reasons:

- Domain or area of work is different:
  - For example, each team is operating in different areas of the code base.
- Skill sets differ:
  - For example, Team A in the previous example is a group of senior engineers who have worked together for years. Team B is a team of interns. People are not fungible resources. They are people who have different skill sets and capabilities.
- Sizing of work differs:
  - We spoke about relative sizing earlier in this section. Sizing of work is one of those measures that is unique to teams. A story point for Team A will be different for Team B.
- Things happen:
  - Stable teams are great in theory, but in practice, teams are dynamic. Whether it's a person retiring, leaving for a new role (or firm), or going on leave for an extended period, our experience is that teams change more often than they don't. A team that has six people at the beginning of the year and six at the end does not mean it was stable.

If you encounter someone pitting teams against each other, try the following antidotes:

- Ask them why—if it's a people manager, encourage them to use metrics as one input to any performance conversation. They should also observe how the team is working together. The team's context is also important.
- If the individual is insistent on using data to compare teams, direct them to value-delivery-focused data such as:
  - Sprint goals (percent of completion before end of sprint; trend over time)
  - Program increment objectives (percent completed before end of program increment; trend over time)

This data will shift the conversation from teams and individuals to value delivery.

THE DATA IS THE WHOLE STORY

Every picture may be worth a thousand words, but is every burn-up chart? If so, a thousand words is not enough to tell the whole story. A classic burn-up chart only tells part of the story. Yes, work got completed on a date. You may even extrapolate how value flowed through the system. (Cumulative flow diagrams are better for visualizing this, by the way.) But this classic vehicle to show project progress leaves out a lot of context. And the business of software development is much more than getting work done. Burn-up charts are numbers on a scale; they don't include what, why, or how work got done. There's likely a great story lurking behind every burn-up chart.

This antipattern is easy for higher level management to fall into. They assume that the data in front of them tell the whole story. Whether it's a burn-up chart or some other set of data showing progress (or lack thereof). They use it to draw conclusions without asking questions to get the big picture. Some of this contextual information is easy to derive. For example, the reason a burn up flatlined in late December is due to everyone being on vacation. Other times, it's less clear. For example, the reason a burn up flatlined for a few weeks is because the continuous integration/continuous delivery (CI/CD) system was completely down. This inhibited moving anything to production.

If you encounter people using metrics data as the entire story, try the following antipattern antidotes:

- Present data with the story—every time—and make it explicit by recording it or writing it down. We have worked with teams where the norm is to show data during sprint review with the demonstration of done work. Don't read out the data in a monotonous tone—"the team finished X items and did not complete X items." Add some color commentary. "The team was able to swarm and get X items finished, but CI/CD problems prevented us from getting the last X over the line." That's a much better (and true) story.
- Coach people on how to analyze sets of data, or interpret data. How should I be looking at this cumulative flow diagram? What

questions should I ask when I see a backlog that has lots of unrefined items in it? Teach people how to fish for themselves, and they will be more educated consumers of data.

MEASURING EVERYTHING (OR NOTHING)

There is no shortage of things to measure in the world of software development. Thanks to modern engineering tooling, we can measure most things that get done, whether it is lines of code written or flow time of work items. Even teams that still use sticky notes and index cards can go measurement crazy.

The two antipatterns worth exploring in this section are mirror opposites. The first is the one where people measure everything. For example, a Scrum Master spends the last day of the sprint assembling spreadsheets of data. They aren't actually using most of the data. But the information might be useful at some point in the future. The other side of this antipattern is the one where people don't measure anything. This could be because a team is new. It could also be because measurement is time intensive (and nobody has the bandwidth to do it). It could also be because the team doesn't know what is worth measuring. These will lead to missed signals and opportunities. Too much data obscures what is important. Too little data (or none) delivers no information to supplement gut feel.

If either of these antipatterns rear their heads, try these antipattern antidotes:

- Determine the audience for the data and engage them about what they actually need to see. Run a goal, question, metric (GQM) session to get stakeholders to determine importance. For example, data that provides the ability to forecast delivery is important. Stakeholders don't care about how many lines of code the team wrote for a story in the current iteration.
- Determine what data are useful for the long term. Software development is rarely a short game, even in organizations that still focus on projects over products. There's a sense that building up

a set of data will be useful to identify areas of future improvement. Examine whether the data you're collecting today are going to make any sort of meaningful impact. If something you're doing now isn't going to have an impact, stop doing it.

- Start using the flow metrics described in this book. This can be in addition to whatever metrics you're already collecting. It can also be in place of whatever metrics you're currently collecting.
- If you find you are not using or discussing them, stop publishing them. If no one complains, stop collecting the information.

INCONSISTENT MEASUREMENT DEFINITIONS

There's only one thing worse than measuring too many or too few things. It's when everyone thinks they're measuring the same thing. But there are subtle—sometimes irreconcilable—differences. This is common when many teams are working towards common goals. The missing ingredient is a common measurement structure. Someone—a program manager, people manager, director—will ask for data about how a team(s) is doing. There will be inconsistencies in data collection and calculation. You'll hear phrases like, "my spreadsheet says that we did X items last week. Why does your spreadsheet say we did N items?"

If inconsistent measurement is constant in your context, try the following antipattern antidotes:

- Create a common definition of the measure and the calculation for the metric.
- Collect all the possible ways that something is being measured, regardless of whether it is right or wrong. Seek to understand how measurement is happening and why it is done that way.
- Convene a discussion to get alignment on data collection—for example, a common understanding of a specific query to use— or an agreement on when to pull data for a given measure.
- Automate as much as possible. After coming to a consensus on what and how to measure, automate it so that inconsistencies can't creep in.

MEASURING HOURS (AND ESTIMATING IN TIME)

"How long is it going to take you to do X?" This is a popular question in the world of software development. The challenge with answering this question is that software creation is variable. Software teams are not making widgets. They're creating valuable functionality, often in complex systems. We've worked with people and teams in the past who have guaranteed that an item would be done within hours—only to have the item take days or weeks to complete, and vice versa. That's the estimation side of hourly measurements.

Asking people on software teams to log time spent on tasks or stories is a popular way to keep track of costs for teams. This is often done to support managing a budget. As organizations shift from a project to product mindset, the funding mindset must shift. Value stream funding is the logical solution. If people are working on one project at a time, hourly billing is easy. You know what team a person works on. "Oh, John is part of the Flamin' Hot Potatoes team that is working on that new installation wizard feature. So, we can bill John's time this week to that feature." In more dynamic environments, allocating time to projects is generally good enough.

If the organization you work with is still tracking hours, try the following antipattern antidotes:

- Ask why—it's possible that the information is for budgeting purposes, but it's also possible that it's "what we've always done," and no longer serves a purpose.
- Shift the focus from tracking hours to value delivery. The flow metrics we describe in this book will help.
- Focus less on precision and more on size. We've worked with successful teams in the past who sized items in hours. The key, though, is that they thought of hours as parts of days. They sliced their work as small as possible. They tried to only have items in their backlog that were about a half day and about a day. That was it. The teams didn't spend time haranguing with each other about whether an item was 17.5 hours or 33.3 hours.

They spent time slicing work as small as possible to aid in value delivery and flow.

- Time accounting is often a reflection of fear that people will not spend enough time working. Focus on measuring the output of teams (use flow metrics) as a replacement for time accounting.

MEASURING THE WRONG THING (AND BELIEVING IT IS RIGHT)

We have worked with teams before who didn't measure anything. When we started to engage with them, we asked them what they thought we should start measuring. We received varying answers. Some teams didn't miss a beat and went right to story point velocity. Other teams were more focused on value delivery. Teams generally need coaching to tie measurements to behaviors they want to promote.

Once teams start measuring, they fall into ruts. They continue to track the things they track, for whatever reasons they track. Suggesting a change in measurement gets viewed with skepticism, doubt, and even fear. The Agile Manifesto preaches finding better ways of working. This insistence to "keep doing what we're doing because it's the right thing to do" is why this is an antipattern.

Teams we have worked with obsess about various measures. *Estimates to actuals* is one; so is tracking hours spent working on bugs. Time spent in meetings is another popular one. All of these are easy to measure, and teams get used to measuring them. These measures might even be useful to fix an occasional problem. But none of these "we've always done it" measures provide information on value delivery.

If your team or organization insists that they are measuring the right thing—and you know they aren't—try the following antipattern antidotes:

- Start collecting measures that you think are worthwhile. Present them to the team as new data, instead of asking to replace whatever data the team likes to see. Offer your analysis of this new data to the team and ask them if they agree with your interpretation.

- Conduct a targeted retrospective on the team's current metrics or bring it up as part of the next regular retrospective. Ask the team where they see future opportunities to improve. Ask whether the existing set of metrics will show whether they are improving (or not).

METRICS FIRE DRILLS

"Get me data on X," shouts the executive to a group of senior leaders. The senior leaders all look at each other. They know very well that they don't have the data that the executive is asking for, but they agree to get the data anyway. This scenario is the dictionary definition of a metrics fire drill.

Getting data from the past can be a tricky proposition. Not all tools lend themselves to aggregating large sets of data. This also assumes data comply with corporate data retention policies and that the system administrator configured the system to collect the data. Another huge challenge with getting data from the past is the loss of context. Data are only part of the story, and collecting and presenting data from the past belie a loss of context.

If you're in the midst of a metrics fire drill, or would like to avoid one, try the following antipattern antidotes:

- Ask why—being asked to go do something is different from knowing why you are doing it. Asking why there is a need to collect something will help bring more context to the request. It might also impact how the collection task ends up happening. Imagine a scenario where someone asks you to collect data that tells you "how long it takes to get stuff done." The immediate reaction might be, "Oh, I'll get them flow time data." But what if "how long it takes to get stuff done" actually meant "how long it takes a customer request to get done"? With that context, lead time is a better measure to surface.

- Be proactive—start talking about data collection when you engage with a new team or organization. Hone in on the metrics that will prove most meaningful, and inspect and adapt.

LOCAL OPTIMIZATION

The impact of measurement is like politics; it's local. The metrics the organization tracks impacts the people doing the work. A common implementation of measurement is early bonus programs. These programs are often based on things like revenue growth and earnings per share. These things seem like they only pertain to the math nerds in the finance department or people in sales. But behind these financial measures is an implicit ask. It is that individuals and teams will build new and enhanced products to achieve those goals. Performance at team level ripples up and down the organizational hierarchy.

We are not advocating for teams to start measuring revenue growth. We can't even think of how you would go about doing that. We're also not advocating that teams ignore the measures that the firm cares about. We have worked with teams blinded by their own local context. They completely forget the larger system. We have seen instances where silos optimize their own metrics at the expense of delivering value to customers. Producing software or enhancements is meaningless if no one is ready to use them—or if sales has no one to sell them to. "Our data looks fantastic. We're beating every measure we set for ourselves and continue to improve." Well, that's a great message to send, but if that message comes at the expense of product delivery, then that is an antipattern.

If you see this antipattern, try these antidotes:

- Talk to the team about how they deliver value. Identify consumers of the work that the team does. Create a diagram that shows the value chain and use it to push the team to think beyond their local context. Examples include: "What do people outside the team need from our team? How are we measuring that now?"

- Have a conversation with the team about how their goals align to company goals. How does their work impact the bottom line?

THE "TRAGEDY OF THE COMMONS"

The "tragedy of the commons" describes self-interested individuals overusing a shared resource. This leads to depletion or degradation of the resource over time. Because nobody owns the resource, there is little incentive for anyone to conserve it. For example, an organization that provides agile coaching to teams without that service will use as much of those people's time as possible. They will always get overwhelmed. Both of us worked in a shared service department where the team was always working at 100 percent capacity. As people got burned out due to overuse, the turnover rate went up. This degraded the efficacy of the shared service at the detriment of everyone who used it. Often, shared services are not measured. If, by some chance they are, the usage rate and who is using the service is not shared.

Very few teams are islands. When teams make decisions, they must make them within the context of the area where they're operating.

If you encounter this antipattern, try these antidotes:

- Map out the value stream that the team operates in. Draw lines between dependencies. Identify required services or people that you involve that are outside of the team. Create metrics that highlight what a team is consuming outside of the team. Use the data in your retrospective. Determine whether you should develop the capability within the team.
- Ask the team to perform Gemba walks—get outside their local context and get a sense of how other teams in their immediate context are using shared resources.
- If you are a shared service team, measure the support you provide and who you are providing it to.

TIME VERSUS PRODUCTIVITY

"Everyone is working overtime, but nothing seems to be getting done."
We have encountered this phrase in our careers. We have even been
the "everyone" in this sentence. At the root of this antipattern is con-
fusing time spent with being productive. You can look back at your
day and point to a bunch of things you did. They may have made you
feel productive, but did it make a real difference or was your day full of
things you had to do as part of your day?

We talk a lot about productivity in the context of value delivery and
customer satisfaction. Value delivery and customer satisfaction tend
to only happen when something is done. Customers are not going to
pay for half-finished software. But how do we measure what teams and
people are doing in the time it takes between the request and value
delivery? Time spent is one thing to measure, but time measurement
assumes that everything we are spending time on is value delivery
centric.

We have seen this antipattern also happen with firms that hire large
batches of contractors. The firm hires them and tells them to go do,
but then comes to find out that there is not much for them to actually
latch on to and do.

If your firm is conflating time with productivity, try these antipattern antidotes:

- Shift the focus to the measurement of value delivery. We've seen
  teams that quantify each backlog item with a business value
  measurement. This measurement helps prioritize what is valuable. Teams measuring the business value of backlog items can
  get a good sense of the value they are delivering.
- Review the backlog to ensure that all work aligns with the delivery of some sort of value. We have worked with firms that
  have tracked time. An underlying reason is that they (i.e., the
  project management office, senior leaders) want to ensure that
  engineers are billing time to high-value work.

- Use function points to measure what is getting delivered using an International Organization for Standardization (ISO) approach.

END-OF-CHAPTER QUESTIONS

Use the following to start a conversation about the contents of this chapter:

1. Which of the antipatterns in this chapter do you currently see in your organization or team?
2. How are you working to resolve the antipatterns that you currently see?
3. What other metrics antipatterns do you see in your organization or team?

Section Three

Introspection

A WORK INTAKE CASE STUDY AS A BUSINESS NOVELLA, CHAPTER 3

It was a crisp fall Saturday outside Dandelion. It's the type of day James would spend hiking in the woods and enjoying a tuna fish sandwich picnic. James, however, was enjoying the faint ozone smell that came from their monitors. James had already mapped how work flows through the organization. Their map included the myriad of people involved in reviewing, influencing, and approving work. It was obvious that there was a problem. No wonder the new product was off target. The big issue was not that there was a problem; rather, it wasn't until Anna felt threatened that anyone took notice. Dandelion was profitable. It was still experiencing some organic growth. Although, much of the growth over the last few years was through acquisition. Most of the people James talked to still didn't see any significant issue. Who cares if it was a bit erratic on delivery? So what if their competitors seemed to be building on better technology? Dandelion could buy them or buy their people. Anna had ended the last session with an ultimatum. James needed data to energize the organization. It was time to pull together some data on flow.

James decided to leverage a hybrid version of flow distribution. Instead of the breakdown outlined in Mik Kersten's *Project to Product*, James gathered information on how the product development parts of the organization budgeted labor spend using some SQL reports from the data warehouse. The data was for the first six months of the fiscal year. The numbers were rough, due to differences in the categorization of labor spend, but they were still useful (see Figure S3.1). Based on budgets and spending, James pieced together a proxy for flow distribution. The data showed that far less was being spent on growing the business and that far more was being spent on running the business. The firm was spending more on the current product suite than the strategic plan for the future. The feeling around the organization that fewer features were being completed was more true than false.

James tried cobbling together a few more metrics before going to catch the last few rays of sunshine. They pulled the list of epics marked *ready for release* (ReR) from the Jira software management program (see Figure S3.2). At Dandelion, ReR is as close to production as any part of the new product. Not exactly *done*, but as good as it currently gets. The data, assuming everyone was keeping up with Jira, was startling. Every development team had been reporting consistent or improving velocity. Yet, the flow of completed features looked like it was being throttled. Work might be getting done, but that work was not translating to completed features.

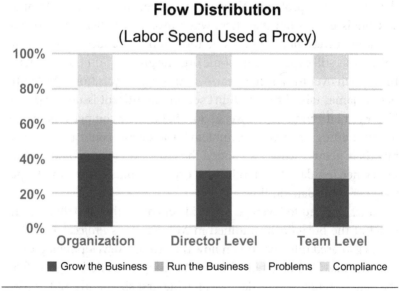

Flow Distribution

Figure S3.1   Flow distribution example.

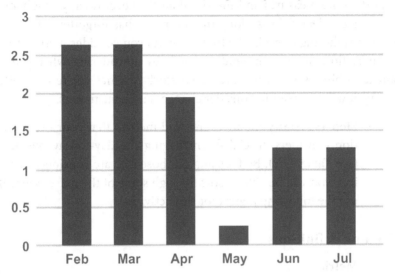

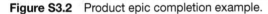

Figure S3.2   Product epic completion example.

The labor data that James could lay hands on wasn't granular enough. It was enough to surmise that the reduction in outcomes correlated with labor spend. Work was getting stuck in the pipeline and then supplanted (or vice versa). Both scenarios cause similar problems. The product, R&D, operations, and delivery groups all used different tracking tools. That meant that no amount of coffee and magic was going to yield even a rough flow-efficiency report. James decided to get a handful of people together on Monday and trace a sample of epics through the system to see if the group could identify bottlenecks.

A more consistent approach to flow metrics would have made short work of the afternoon. But at least James had data. Even if it wasn't perfect, it was telling a story.

EXECUTING NEW IDEAS

As James's saga presses forward, now it is your turn to consider metrics. All useful metrics are supposed to be tools to provide structured transparency. Almost every organization that we have worked with reports more measures and metrics than they ever do anything with. Some get collected for so long that everyone has forgotten why they started gathering them in the first place. As you consider metrics that support flow, we recommend to begin by considering what you're already doing. Once you have taken stock of what you're currently doing, it will be easier to consider changes and adjustments.

- **Step 1:** Identify the measures and metrics that your organization considers crucial for managing the day-to-day business (see Table S3.1). By focusing on those that are considered critical, you will be able to sort through some of the noise. We will use the following matrix for this activity.

Column definitions

- **Metric**
  - □ This is the name of the metric. It could be one of the flow metrics we discussed in this section or one you're already using.
- **Audience**
  - □ This is to convey which type of people care about this metric. Think about the organizational chart activity in *Section Two's Introspection.*
- **Now?**
  - □ This is a simple yes/no question: "Are you using this metric now?"
- **How?**
  - □ This is for logging how you are going to get the metric. A common answer to this question might be something like "Jira."
- **Level**
  - □ This ties metrics into the three levels that we've talked about throughout this book.

Table S3.1 Metrics that Matter

Metric	Audience	Now?	How?	Level	Value

- **Value**
  - □ This is the clincher—"Why?"—if you will. This should get you thinking about how this metric delivers value to the organization, product/department, and/or team.

Capture the current measures and metrics in the previously shown matrix, with the exception of the *Value* column. Feel free to add rows if needed.

- **Step 2:** After creating an inventory of your current metrics, reflect on the table. How many measures and metrics are focused on the category of information (status, budget, predicted completion, etc.)? Are there candidates for consolidation?
- **Step 3:** Complete the value column for each metric. Are there metrics that have tenuous value propositions? Should some metrics be marked for elimination?
- **Step 4:** What information is missing that would allow you to answer whether you are working on the right mix of work and whether it is flowing in a consistent, predictable fashion?

Section Four

Section Four

Work Intake Problems and Solutions

Section Contents

SECTION INTRODUCTION

Work intake problems are common. So common, in fact, that you might suspect that you could copy and paste a solution from a blog entry or book. The resolution, though, is not that simple. Most work intake problems are observable at the team level. Yet, they often stem from systemic problems in middle management (or above). More complexity occurs when root causes combine, reflecting organizational culture and design. Recognizing the base problem is the first step in cutting the Gordian Knot of work intake down to something more manageable.

21

THE PRIMARY CAUSES OF
WORK INTAKE PROBLEMS

> **Learning Objectives**—by the end of this chapter, you will be able to:
> - Describe the primary causes of work intake problems
> - Understand the types of questions you can use to assess what types of primary causes exist
> - Recognize potential solutions to common work intake problems

There are eight common causes for work intake problems. These causes often occur in tandem with one another. They are always a reflection of organizational culture. Culture, in this case, is a shorthand way to say chosen behavior. Knowing the primary causes of work intake problems is useful. People's motivations are not always obvious, though. Recognition requires conversation, observation, and experimentation.

The following sections outline the most common causes of work intake problems—including hints for recognizing them. Before we dive in, remember that even though the causes are common, it does not mean they are easy to solve.

CAUSE #1: GOAL CONFLICT

Goal conflict is the single most prevalent reason for work intake problems. A typical conflict occurs because teams want to complete work in an orderly manner, while someone else wants a piece of work done right now. Everyone perceives their reason to be rational. It does not matter whether it's planned work, ad hoc, based on a contract, an emergency, or an evolutionary change; no one is acting irrationally based on their business goals. The outcome of conflicting goals is that teams will often accept work they had not planned. Acceptance is either overt or covert. For example, if a team is using Scrum, the sprint backlog is not a revolving door. The framework requires tacit agreement that the sprint backlog will not change until the next sprint planning event.

Some of the types of problems caused by goal conflict include:

- Failure to meet goals—for example, sprint goals in Scrum
- Team frustration
- Employee turnover
- Angry stakeholders (when their work gets delayed)

Questions to use when evaluating whether goal conflict is occurring include:

- Do team members, managers, or executives value different time horizons?
- Are there different perspectives on what market the product is serving?
- When goal conflict occurs, is there an incentive to compromise or adopt a middle ground?
- Is there trust between team members or teams?
- Are disagreements and arguments about approaches common?

The goals of people, teams, and organizations have a huge impact on their behavior. Identifying differences in goals is one of the missions of all leaders.

CAUSE #2: NEED OUTSTRIPS SUPPLY

Need outstripping supply comes in two basic versions. The version you're living depends on whether you recognize it is happening.

The first version occurs when requests continue to outweigh the ability to deliver, but not by enough where people realize it. In this scenario, the backlog grows faster than work is being completed. The metaphor to describe this scenario is boiling frogs. They don't notice the rising temperature and react until it is too late. As backlog growth outweighs delivery, stakeholders feel the group is letting them down. They perceive the group as slow, lazy, or inefficient. This causes them to begin to grumble. A common reaction is for the team to address the problem by overcommitting. They see overperformance as a way to get back into good graces. This approach might work in the short run, but in the long term, the stress on the team and stakeholders will reduce effectiveness. It will drive up quality problems, turnover, and cost.

Some of the types of problems caused when need outstrips supply include:

- Increased technical debt
- Slow delivery of functionality
- Quality problems
- Frustration—both for teams and stakeholders
- Employee turnover

The second version occurs when people recognize the need/supply imbalance. They use it to generate fear and stress. Teams or organizations attempt to overcommit and overperformance occurs. They generate the same issues as the unrecognized imbalance; but they do so with deeper and fiercer reactions by all those involved.

In this case, some of the types of problems caused include:

- Low psychological safety
- Slow delivery of functionality
- Team infighting

- Frustration—both for teams and stakeholders
- Employee turnover

Questions to use when evaluating whether need/supply mismatches are occurring include:

- Does the amount of work added to the backlog more or less equal the work that is being delivered?
- Do people complain (more) about the ability to deliver value in a timely way?
- Is there pressure for work to jump the queue?
- Are team members complaining about the amount of work others on the team are doing?
- Are the number of delivered defects increasing?

Recognized or unrecognized need/supply mismatches are easy to diagnose. Remember that need will always outstrip supply to some extent. The size of the gap and the reactions to the perceived gap are what generate behavioral problems.

CAUSE #3: PAY PRACTICES

How leaders get paid is a specialized version of the goal conflict cause. Many organizations leverage performance pay structures tied to short-term outcomes. For example, hitting sales goals or reducing outstanding change requests are short-term outcomes. These outcomes are sometimes outside the boundaries of sustainable performance. They are often couched as *stretch goals*. We've seen teams scramble and sacrifice to meet quarterly goals, only to face technical debt and rework problems at the beginning of the next period. Short-term thinking often conflicts with long-term plans. This causes leaders to ignore guardrails—the same guardrails that keep them from interrupting the agreed-upon flow of work.

In this instance, some of the types of problems caused include:

- Hiding work
- Conflicts between executives, product owners, managers, and teams

Questions to use when evaluating whether pay practice issues are occurring include:

- Is there too much focus on short-term requirements?
- Are mid- or long-term technical architecture needs addressed in a timely way?
- When you ask about pay practices, are there significant short-term bonuses?
- Is the team turnover higher than other organizations in the area?

The impact of pay practices on work intake is the hardest category to diagnose. This is because asking about how people get paid is often difficult. Even if you're able to get answers through the grapevine, they may be speculative in nature. But this impact is often easy to infer after the fact. For example, Tom has worked for several firms that had large sales quotas. The pressure to slip in enhancements and tweaks always went up in the fourth quarter of each year. Salespeople were trying to make sales to meet their quotas.

CAUSE #4: PROJECT THINKING VERSUS PRODUCT THINKING

A project mindset is a paradigm whereby funding is tied to the delivery of specific functionality. And when that funding runs out, so does the ability to get any more work done. Project stakeholders perceive that they only get one bite at the proverbial apple. Thus, everything has to be the top priority, even if it is unplanned.

A product mindset, though, is a paradigm whereby funding exists for a pipeline of work. This could be features, functions, enhancements, or technical debt reduction. Product thinkers do not see the current work as their only opportunity to have work done on their behalf. Instead of funding based on the delivery of specific functionality, funding is a *bucket*. The product manager or product owner bases use of funds on their changing understanding of stakeholder, customer, and market needs.

In this situation, some of the types of problems caused include:

- Infighting (for people and funding)
- Delays
- Overutilization of people

The type of perspective a firm has toward work can be determined based on the words and phrases people use, as well as the funding approach used for work.

Questions to determine whether product thinking and project thinking collisions are occurring include:

- Do people call all (or a majority of) work *projects*?
- Do people refer to teams as *product teams* or *project teams*?
- Do team members have roles that include the words *project* or *program*?
- Do people refer to defined scope and budget?
- Does running a project confer special authority and responsibilities compared to other work?
- Is work driven from a fixed requirements document?
- Are individual initiatives funded?
- Do projects impacting a specific product have a different product owner?

CAUSE #5: URGENCY/IMPORTANCE DICHOTOMY

Urgency is the person who yells the loudest. Importance is the impact on, or the amount of, business value delivered. Those who yell the loudest generally trump those who lead with business value. At least until those businesses fail.

Problems are one area where importance and urgency often intersect. When production is down and clients are upset, "We'll get to that next sprint" is usually career-limiting. While important, this type of interruption has all the same negative side effects. Yet, the value of fixing high-priority problems generally trumps the problems caused—at least in the short term.

Some of the types of problems caused by urgency/importance include:

- Doing the wrong work
- Doing the right work at the wrong time

Questions to use when evaluating whether urgency is trumping importance include:

- Is there a process for prioritizing all work?
- Are there standard criteria for prioritizing work?
- Are standard criteria for prioritizing work always used?
- Is there an operational definition of business value in use?

Teams that jump when someone raises their voice are teams that react to the urgent at the expense of what is important.

CAUSE #6: CLASSES OF SERVICE

Classes of service are a way to deal with work that enters with a different priority or urgency than other work. Many kanban implementations have a swimlane for expedited work. This is a class of service. Examples of expedited work include significant defects. It also might include that special piece of work that the CEO wants. This approach causes work intake problems because it causes interruption problems. Work gets sorted by priority, and then adjusted when a higher priority piece appears. When expedited work interrupts planned work, it causes ripples, and it stops or slows down planned and committed work.

Some types of problems caused when work is expedited include:

- Everything except the expedited item is later than it needs to be or should be
- Cheating on work intake processes by jumping the queue

Questions to determine if classes of service are causing work intake problems include:

- Does the team's board or program's board have identified classes of service?

- Is work delayed because other work is being injected into the timebox?
- Do team members or stakeholders ask for work to get expedited in order only to get it started?

Diagnosing whether classes of service exist is usually simple. Look at the team or program's board. Less explicit implementations are harder to diagnose. For example, "Oh, right—that's the item that the CEO said we need to do now."

Experience Report

Kanban Without an Expedite Lane

Including a lane at the top of a kanban for expedited work is a common implementation of classes of service. But does every kanban board have to include this by default? Isn't including this on a board an invitation for use and abuse? Jeremy worked with a kanban team that was supporting custom software implementations. Every Monday, he would meet with a handful of folks. This included the managers of the people fixing and enhancing the software. It also included the people in the field who were installing and troubleshooting the software. The goal of the meeting was to examine work in progress and determine the next five items to put in the to-do list from the backlog. The list allowed no more than five items. Priority was top-down. There was no expedite lane on the board. The team was using Trello, a workflow management tool, and at the time, there was no concept of swimlanes in Trello. Had there been an expedite lane, there would have been items that were a fit for it. But these were issues injected into the team. The team was supporting customers, and installers encountered urgent issues during upgrades. But the team knew the upgrade schedule. They could limit the to-do list during those weeks in case any issues arose during the upgrade. Issues that came up during upgrades resulted in calls between installers and team members. Time was of the essence. There was no ability or desire to have a lane on a board to address these requests. If the issue led to a software change request, the team would capture those on the board for visibility, and they would go at the top of the priority list. While an expedite concept did exist within this team for in-the-moment issues, it never existed on the team's kanban board.

CAUSE #7: CONTROL

One of Dante's nastier levels of hell is for people who force teams to take work when it is clear that they can't absorb it. This controlling behavior makes work late, reduces quality, and causes turnover—or worse, it creates demoralized developers who stay and poison the well.

Some of the types of problems caused by a lack of control include:

- Quality problems
- Late work
- Frustration
- Employee turnover
- Passive aggressiveness

Questions that will help to determine if there are control issues include:

- What do interactions between leaders, stakeholders, and team members say about leadership tactics?
- Are people or teams always told what to do and how to do it?
- Is there only one leader in all situations?

Leaders of all types can exhibit micromanagement or command-and-control approaches. Long-term use of these approaches has deleterious effects on teams and team members.

CAUSE #8: "YES-ITIS"

This single word—"yes"—is at the root of most work intake problems. This is because leaders or teams want to please their clients and stakeholders. A better way to think of this problem is as the inability to say "no." Whether it's due to an overriding need to please or a lack of power, if "yes" is the only response you give to the question of whether to do new work, your backlog will be overrun. You will start everything and finish very little. No one will be happy, including you.

Some of the types of problems caused by *yes-itis* include:

- Delays
- Quality problems

- Technical debt
- Destruction of trust

Questions to help identify if "yes" is a proverbial 4-letter word include:

- When replying to a request to do new work, is "The team will get right on it!" the correct answer? (This includes any other variation of "yes.")
- Does saying that work will go on the backlog guarantee it will get done (and soon)?
- Does saying that work will go on the backlog guarantee that the requestor will not ever hear about the item again?
- When was the last piece of work started and then canceled?
- Does the team or organization measure cycle time?
- Is cycle time important?

Diagnosing *yes-itis* requires listening to the transactions that are occurring at the work intake interface.

You Asked . . .

"Saying *yes* to things is part of the company culture. I literally can't say *no!*" We've both worked with companies that have their vision and mission written on the walls of the office. Both explain the company culture in great, aspirational detail. They even include sets of core principles. They haven't said that employees must stop the thing they are working on when a new request comes in. People—ourselves included—have perceived *yes-itis* to be the culture. They have interpreted the culture as one in which saying "yes" to work gets equated with being a team player (or even nice). The irony is that the behavior of saying "yes" erodes a lot of the other things we have seen in those artifacts. For example, if your company strives to provide customers with the best product, your company will not be able to deliver on that promise if your engineers keep saying "yes" to whatever work sidles up to their desks.

A FINAL WORD ON CAUSES

The primary causes of work intake problems are common. Many organizations and leaders have internalized and normalized them. They are sometimes even celebrated. (Yes, we have seen people get promoted for following antipatterns!) Those leaders are not evil; they simply think that this is the way work should get done. They fail to realize that accepting any of these causes will lead to nasty results in the long run. Doing so creates a hot mess that is often solved only by hitting the reset button on the organization—or at least a significant portion of the leadership.

END-OF-CHAPTER QUESTIONS

Use the following to start a conversation about the contents of this chapter:

1. Which of the causes of work intake problems have you seen?
2. How did you recognize the cause?
3. How did you communicate the problem and cause to others?

This book has free material available for download from the
Web Added Value™ resource center at *www.jrosspub.com*

22

FIXING THE PRIMARY CAUSES
OF WORK INTAKE PROBLEMS

> **Learning Objectives**—by the end of this chapter, you will be able to:
> - Describe the fixes for the eight primary causes of work intake problems
> - Describe which fixes address which causes

The majority of work intake problems are resolvable by using one or more of the fixes in this chapter. The causes of work intake problems often occur in clusters. This is because they reflect organizational structure, culture, funding, and methodologies. You will have to address more than one root cause. Remember—recognition of the problem is the first step in eventual resolution.

FIX #1: STAFFING LEVELS

This is always the first thing leaders try when attempting to fix work intake problems. It is rarely the right answer. This fix only addresses the scenario where need outstrips supply. With that said, having more than enough people can mask all sorts of problems for a period of time. Adding more people is not a long-term fix. It will not make a difference if a team or organization is not controlling the amount of work they take. Adding people is also not a good idea if "yes" is the only answer to the will-you-do-it question. You can add people to cover a problem in the short run, but adding people sends the message that covering up problems is acceptable. This means that the culture favors urgency over importance. This is the death knell for innovation.

Causes addressed:

- Need outstrips supply (Version 1)

This is almost always the first solution people try. We challenge you to try one or two other solutions first.

Facilitating This Fix

If the number of people is your issue, here are some thoughts on how to facilitate this fix:

1. Develop a quantitative understanding of the value stream or teams' capacity.
   - Start by collating historical data:
     - Median throughput
     - Flow distribution
     - Entry and exit lines from the team or value stream's cumulative flow diagram
   - Use this data to understand current and future capacity (trend). Also, look at whether the backlog is shrinking or growing. Combining this data will indicate whether you need more people. It will also show how much the capacity has to increase to achieve equilibrium.
2. Understand how long it takes to onboard new people/teams. Adding people in knowledge work does not lead to an immediate increase in capacity.
   - Interview the newest people to the firm:

- How long did it take them to get up to speed with how the firm develops products? Was the onboarding process adequate? What changes would they make to the process? Use this knowledge to streamline the process. Make someone responsible for making the on-boarding process work.
- Determine if the time you need to onboard supports your product/project roadmap. Do this before adding anyone as full-time employees or contractors. Bringing in new people only to have demand fall (and then have to fire people) is a waste of time and goodwill.
  - Determine whether to add full-time employees or contractors. Or if a mix is appropriate.
  - Do you need effective people right now? Or do you have the luxury of developing skills over time? Is the change in staffing only temporary to handle a big influx of work? Or will the demand for work in this area remain steady? What kind of budget do you have to hire? If you are bringing in long-term contractors, identify a path to bring the knowledge in-house. Do this through a contract-to-hire arrangement or create a plan to develop the skills in-house.

FIX #2: ALIGNMENT

Alignment can be an easy fix if the culture allows transparency. In cases where many organizations work together, they must agree on shared goals. Define success so that "all for one and one for all" is not only a line from *The Three Musketeers*.

Causes addressed:

- Goal conflict
- Urgency—importance dichotomy (at least in part)
- Classes of service

Where transparency is difficult, consider the radical approach of adopting transparency. It's the first step in any solution. We often find that making work visible creates energy that can translate into change.

Facilitating This Fix

Here are some thoughts on how to facilitate this fix:

1. Adopt shared goals
   - Identify leadership's core goal—the *Commander's Intent*[21] (CI). The CI clearly defines the end state for the product, program, or team. It is the basis for developing shared goals and planning.
   - Conduct a workshop for the team, program, or organization to create a shared set of goals. Creating goals that support the CI as a group promotes buy-in from all parties.
2. Maximize visibility
   - Assess whether teams have the information they need to make decisions. Questions to assess include:
     - Are shared goals and CI understood by team members?
     - Are goals and plans visible to leaders outside the team or program?
     - Do leaders and team members share the same goals?
     - What knowledge needs compartmentalization?

   Be thoughtful in scenarios where any one group *sees* more data than the other. Analyze the risk of sharing information. Create mitigation plans for information that isn't shared (or can't be).

---

[21] Heath, Chip and Heath, Dan. *Made to Stick: Why Some Ideas Survive and Others Die*, Random House, New York, NY, 2007, p. 26.

3. Standardize measurement
   - Take stock of the success measures in use across the organization. See where there's inconsistency. Conduct conversations or workshops to sync to common definitions and measurement approaches. Automate data collection. Humanize analysis of data.

FIX #3: CHANGE THE METHODS OF WORKING

The classic project management perspective approach is to fund, monitor, and deliver work. Breaking this paradigm requires change. It requires supporting departments as work flows through the value stream. A product perspective requires coupling funding and value delivery. There is no explicit funding end date. Backlogs get built and prioritized based on value. Funding lasts until one of two things occurs: either the work on the backlog no longer meets the required rate of return or doing something else will deliver more value.

Causes addressed:

- Project thinking versus product thinking
- Classes of service

Facilitating This Fix

Here are some thoughts on how to facilitate this fix:

1. Create a portfolio kanban
   - Prioritize and fund features (or programs) with full transparency.
   - Techniques that create value-based competition (like an internal "Shark Tank") are useful. Facilitate and monitor competitive techniques so they do not generate bad behavior.
   - Create a culture where funding gets pulled from low-value work.

2. Leverage value chains
   - Identify and organize to support value chains. A value chain depicts the steps a firm takes to deliver value to customers.
   - Measure and manage flow using flow metrics. Work that has not reached its intended customer is inventory and potential waste.
3. Stop using classes of service
   - Stop (or curtail) the use of classes of service. Classes of service foster an interrupt-driven culture that makes teams unpredictable.
   - For any class of service that you keep, consider the following questions:
     - Are the classes of service formal or informal? (An informal approach is actually back door work intake.)
     - How often are they used? If more than once in a while, you may have a planning issue or someone with too much privilege.

Classes of service are a way to deal with an organizational problem without addressing the root cause. Address the root cause.

FIX #4: ACQUIRING CAPABILITIES

Being able to do the work is not always a function of having the right number of bodies. It is more a function of having the right skills. When a team has a deficit in the capabilities needed to get a job done, they either have to build or acquire skills. Consider building a technical profile of the team. Then, project what that profile needs to look like in the future. The difference provides a roadmap to build the team.

Causes addressed:

- Need outstrips supply (Version 1)
- Project thinking versus product thinking

Managing and building skills on a team is table stakes for decent management. If you are a manager, team lead, or a Scrum Master, write "build team capabilities" on the top of your to-do list. Do something about it daily.

Facilitating This Fix

Here are some thoughts on how to facilitate this fix:

1. Understand how your company handles employee development
   - Get out your employee handbook and read it, then go to HR and validate the organization's philosophy.
2. Establish organizational training
   - Establish a proactive culture—identify needed capabilities and put programs in place to develop those capabilities.
3. Skills inventory with gaps
   - Develop a skills heatmap to identify expertise. Compare expertise to needs to establish gaps. Create a heatmap by making a table that lists necessary skills down the left side and the names of people across the top. Ask each person to rate themselves on a scale as to how proficient they are. The gaps will be obvious.
   - Work with leadership to develop a plan to fill the gaps through hiring, renting (contractors), training, or shifting people. This should be a periodic activity that has a proactive component. Otherwise, longer term options such as people development will not be useful.
4. Make skill set development easy
   - Build it into how people are already working. Pair programming is one tried-and-true way to make this happen. So is encouraging people to take on work that isn't in their typical skill set. Even if the capacity of the team/program decreases, it will only be temporary. The result is worth it.

FIX #5: CULTURE

Culture is the beliefs, behaviors, and shared experiences that shape how team members or a company's employees interact. Examples of culture include:

- Pay practices
- Tolerance of interruptions
- Definition of work as important or urgent
- Treatment of people who challenge the status quo

Culture is a reflection of a team's and an organization's habits and memories. Culture change demands the building of new habits and memories. Implement the change and push people to hold the line until new habits and guardrails begin to form. For example, if teams have *yes-itis*, implement a policy that all work has to be on the backlog. It must then get prioritized by the team before starting.

   Causes addressed:

- Need outstrips supply (Version 2)
- Pay practices
- Control
- Yes-itis
- Classes of service

Culture—how a team or organization chooses to act—is the last fix to try in almost every case. This is because it is hard and politically dangerous. In the end, changing behavior (not even belief) is always the most effective. None of the other fixes can happen unless behavior changes. Tackling work intake problems caused by mistakes or technical issues can be easy. But most of the problems boil down to culture. Culture change requires drawing hard lines; then holding to those lines until the new behavior becomes second nature. This might sound draconian, but the risk to the business is too high to let work hit the team in a haphazard way. You have to fake it until you make it.

Facilitating This Fix

Here are some thoughts on how to facilitate this fix:

1. Establish centralized guardrails
    - Guardrails are the guidelines, practices, and constraints that are put in place to ensure that people follow certain standards, achieve quality, and maintain consistency. Guardrails are a formal instantiation of culture. Centralizing guardrails ensures that team behaviors do not vary outside of norms. Guardrails include things like:
        □ Security requirements
        □ Testing approaches
        □ Approaches to flow
        □ Methods and frameworks
        □ Continuous integration/continuous delivery approaches
        □ Commitment to continuous improvement

        One example of a guardrail is the Scaled Agile Framework® *Program Predictability Measure*. This measures the actual business value delivery over the course of each program increment. The guardrail for this measure is 80–100 percent. Another example of a guardrail is the norm of frowning upon having to work over a weekend.
2. Respect the guardrails
    - Guardrails are only useful if people care about them. Getting people to care about guardrails is not easy. It requires constant messaging from leaders about why the guardrails exist. Leaders must also be clear that violating guardrails on purpose is unacceptable.

A FINAL WORD ON FIXES

The causes of work intake problems are diagnosable, but only if you are willing to expend a bit of shoe leather talking with team members and stakeholders. Sometimes, you don't even need to do that much walking around; listen to the conversations in the hall, elevator, or as people are queuing for coffee. Knowing that there is a problem is important. The hard part starts when you try to fix the problem or problems.

END-OF-CHAPTER QUESTIONS

Use the following to start a conversation about the contents of this chapter:

1. How many of the fixes described in this section have you tried? What were the results?
2. How have others tried to fix the work intake problems described in this chapter?

23

WHY MIDDLE MANAGEMENT CAN BE *MUSHY*

Learning Objectives—by the end of this chapter, you will be able to:
- Define why middle management can be mushy
- Describe what roles are active in the middle
- Describe work intake in the middle

We thought a lot about how to describe what we see happening in the middle level of companies. This is where the information that agilists preach gets misconstrued, misaligned, hijacked, circumvented, or ignored. How your company deals with this level—or doesn't—will be a huge factor in how much value you get from agile. This is because decisions at this level have a major impact on the proverbial atomic unit of agile—the team. This territory can often be ambiguous and complex. There are no clear *by-the-book* answers in sight. We thought that *mushy* summed things up well.

WHAT IS THE MIDDLE?

The middle levels of all companies are areas of transition. Input from the top gets translated into action at the lower levels. This translation requires interpretation and change. Creating change means building alliances, making deals, and selling ideas. These layers also mark the transition between doing, managing, and administration. This is one of the central career ladders within every organization. Organizational politics plays a role in both types of transitions. The idea of organizational politics might feel smarmy, but it seems to be part of the human DNA. Instead of avoiding it, we should focus on using it for positive purposes. This includes building alliances, making deals, and selling ideas. Politics can be a tool to improve how we work and to increase the value we deliver.

You Asked . . .

Is there a word other than "politics" we can use to describe some of what happens in the middle?

If the word *politics* makes you feel smarmy, try using the word *influence* instead. Change agents use many influence strategies to make change happen and then stick. Change agents rarely come with job titles that convey authority, like Director, VP, or CEO. We have rarely worked with people in these capacities that we would consider true change agents. Therefore, if politics seems like a word you'd rather not use, call yourself an influencer.

WHO IS ACTIVE IN THE MIDDLE?

Many roles can be active in the middle levels of an organization. It depends on the size and composition of a company. That is yet another reason why this level can be so complex. There are so many people and roles active at this level.

The middle often includes all of the following roles:

- Process focused
  - Agile coach
  - Scrum Master
  - Project manager
  - Program manager
- Product focused
  - Product owner
  - Product manager
  - Sales managers
  - Marketing managers
  - Customer-facing internal stakeholders (i.e., sales, marketing, technical support)
- Management focused
  - Director
  - Senior manager
  - Manager
  - Team lead

WORK INTAKE IN THE MIDDLE

Work that enters the middle does not need the whole enterprise to deliver. Yet, the work is still greater than a single team. Some companies will refer to the work that is between the strategic and tactical as features. Others use terms like epics, programs, or projects. We are going to use the term product to refer to this type of work. The assumption we are making is that to complete this type of work, a company is going to have more than one team working on it over some modicum of time (multiple months, several sprints, etc.).

A Common Path Through the Middle

The common path for work intake in this middle layer starts in the same way as the happy path, described in Chapter 2. An enterprise-sized piece of work gets decomposed into divisional or department-sized pieces. Then, each department or division pulls its work. The distinction between pull and push is unclear at this level. Once the work is in the hands of middle managers, it gets broken down into smaller chunks. Then the fun starts. As work gets decomposed, the opportunities for dysfunction start to show up. The whole reason for breaking work down is to facilitate it going to different teams or parts of a company. That way, the enterprise-sized piece can get done in short order. This is a classic scaling strategy. A major problem with this strategy is cohesion. When a large piece of work becomes lots of little pieces it loses cohesion. Hence, the need for coordination by a Program Management Office (PMO). Even with a PMO involved, communication and coordination isn't easy. With work in different backlogs, both are more difficult. Each team prioritizes using different biases, principles, and context. "It's like herding cats" is a common refrain we hear in these scenarios. Organizations spend lots of time and effort getting large work efforts to completion. Agile Release Trains from the Scaled Agile Framework® are an approach to this challenge. A PMO is an example of a group that exists to shepherd large work efforts.

Example: "Let's Go to the Cloud!"

At the annual company meeting, the CEO announces that the focus of the next fiscal year is to migrate the company's product suite to the Cloud. "We're going to be in the Cloud before the end of the year!" There's a huge round of applause from everyone at the announcement. But once the cheers die down, the leaders in the room start to think. They aren't sure how that mission is going to jibe with the other high-priority work in their backlogs.

Days later, leaders finally receive something practical to work with. A large chunk of work shows up in the company's software change system. It includes supporting, high-level documentation. This new enterprise backlog item includes the migration order of specific products. This is the first layer of decomposition of the high-level "Going to the Cloud" initiative. These smaller pieces can then get pulled (or pushed) into the areas of the company that support specific products.

For this example, let's focus on the first product that is set for migration to the Cloud, known as *Alpha*. The CEO believes existing and new customers could derive immediate value from it being Cloud-based. The Sales group has made a big point that they could sell more business if only Alpha was in the Cloud. Cloud aside, existing customers are clamoring for other enhancements to the existing product. These enhancements are in a lengthy backlog of product enhancements. Going to the Cloud will solve very few of the items in the backlog. The growth of the list of enhancement requests shows no sign of slowing. The middle managers know that moving Alpha to the Cloud is not going to be enough for existing customers. It also won't change their expectations around receiving a steady stream of enhancements.

Imagine you are a middle manager for Alpha. Your main task in this example is not helping do the work. It's not helping prioritize the work. Your main task is helping the product teams that report to you navigate these waters. You want to do the work that supports the CEO's vision and company's mission, but you have to balance the lofty corporate mission with your current reality. Your reality begins with your two teams of seven people each. None of those people have worked on Cloud-based products. There is also no clear guidance on who is building the infrastructure that will host Alpha in the Cloud. Your e-mail box is full of open technical questions. You also know there is a significant backlog of actionable work for paying customers. It is targeted for the existing non-Cloud version of the product, but it's still ready. Any work done on the current platform, though, will have to go to the Cloud-based platform.

We could continue ratcheting up the layers of complexity in the example, but we'll refrain. You can see that there are significant mismatches. Some of the mismatches include:

- The teams do not currently have the skill set to do the work.
- The priority of getting the product into the Cloud is high for the company; yet, there is more preparation needed before teams can start doing the work. Saying "take our product to the Cloud" is too amorphous.

- There are outstanding technical considerations that are not solved. Teams do not have the organizational authority to make technical infrastructure decisions. These must happen before moving forward.
- When work is ambiguous or stalled due to indecision, middle managers will not wait to act. They will instead focus on the stakeholders that are yelling the loudest. In our example, stakeholders will be yelling about the backlog for existing customers.

This example highlights the types of challenges that middle management must address. They must organize the intersection between people, resources, and client needs. The end result is that everyone is (sort of) happy.

END-OF-CHAPTER QUESTIONS

Use the following to start a conversation about the contents of this chapter:

1. How many people are in the middle of your company?
2. What are the names of the roles that are active in the middle of your company?
3. How does work enter the middle of your company?
4. How many organizational layers are there between teams and the CEO role?
5. What is the typical span of control for middle managers?
6. How many geographies are in the middle of your company?

24

MIDDLE MANAGEMENT ANTIPATTERNS: COMPETING INTERESTS

Learning Objectives—by the end of this chapter, you will be able to:
- Describe a competing interest
- Recognize competing interest antipatterns
- Effectively resolve competing interest antipatterns

Middle management is *mushy* because of the presence of competing interests. As agilists, we love to preach the gospel of alignment. It is a valuable concept that many of us bring to the companies where we work. It can be getting aligned around a piece of work or around a common set of priorities. The challenge is that some in the middle level put their own interests above the organization's. This happens no matter how many times we say "alignment," bring visibility to the lack of it, or conduct workshops seeking to get it. Work that enters this level must navigate this labyrinthine web of competing interests. These competing interests could be hierarchical, technical, or some other reason. The work itself ends up taking a back seat to the needs and egos of individuals. The fallout from these competing interests lands on the teams executing the work. Teams can become confused, apathetic, or generally misaligned when the middle gets mushy.

HIERARCHICAL INTERESTS

Almost every company has an organizational chart, and, by proxy, a hierarchy. We advocate for things like self-direction and autonomy at work. But if the CEO calls you up and asks you to do something, you are going to do it as fast as possible.

Managers, senior managers, directors, and team leads inhabit the middle. People in this level have often been in management for five or more years. Depending on who you ask, they have anywhere from eight to ten or one to six direct reports. Many companies hire from within for middle management positions. That means middle managers have roots in the delivery aspects of the organization. The following sections are examples of how hierarchies cause work intake problems in the middle of organizations.

Example—The New Manager

A team member was recently promoted to manager of the team. The team member was an essential, albeit opinionated, technical contributor. Since the promotion, this person has taken a more forceful role when the team has planned their work. He has even gone as far as rearranging the priority list based on what he thinks the priority should be. There are customer-facing enhancements on the backlog. There are also items related to organizational initiatives. Both types of items often fall behind the new manager's priorities.

The manager takes over the responsibility for triaging work. The manager determines what to do, picks out which team member(s) will do it, and assigns it.

The manager controls everything about work intake for the team. He dictates the list of priorities, triages work, establishes solutions, and assigns the work. His promotion is a sign that he knows what he is doing. The needs of the manager take precedent over the needs of the team members, the work, and the organization's customers. This is a common pattern. Most organizations promote people to management based on technical acumen. They do nothing to train them on being leaders.

Example—The Loudest Voice

A solution architect (SA) decides that she needs to control work intake. She wants to be sure the application evolves according to her vision. This SA was a founding member of the firm and has a deep relationship with one of the primary customers. Her longevity and relationship with the customer have earned her political power. She is heard above all others. The primary customer is happy, but other customers are beginning to grumble. This scenario is dangerous in the long term. It de-emphasizes the impact of roles like product owner or product manager.

A variant of this scenario is in the following experience report. In it, the loudest voice generates organizational power by creating a key-person risk. This puts the organization and product at risk.

Experience Report

The Loudest Voice—Right at the Top

Both authors worked at a firm that still employed many of its original employees. These employees had put their blood, sweat, and tears into starting and growing the firm. Many of them had risen to positions of authority—C-level, VP-level, and director-level. It was a technology firm. Because of this, the software development organization had significant political power. The chief technology officer (CTO) was one of the founding developers and led software development. The CTO used each month's department meeting as a bully pulpit to control work intake. The CTO would identify new initiatives, adjust priorities, and assign teams new work. The communication was one way. This led to great focus, but also reduced empowerment and critical thought by the staff.

Antipattern Antidotes

Here are some thoughts on how to resolve this antipattern:

- Establish clear roles
  - Explicitly identify the responsibilities of each role in the work intake equation. Where there are deviations from the organizational norms, document those differences. For example, the product owner in Scrum is often an adjunct to roles like manager, director, or team lead. The role doesn't have hierarchical authority to set priorities. The role definition grants that authority.
- Educate senior leaders on work intake processes
  - Train all leaders in their work intake roles. Do not expect anyone to absorb new behaviors from watching a video or reading an e-mail. Anyone who does not understand a process will fall back on what has made them successful in the past.
- Coach
  - Provide collaborative support to leaders. Help them succeed as they participate in the work intake process. Empathetic feedback accentuates good practices and nips poor practices in the proverbial bud.
  - Consider developing an empathy map. Craft it for a generic leader in each of the major levels of the organization. This will help anyone who is trying to improve work intake to understand the needs and desires of the people they interact with.

TECHNICAL INTERESTS

Many of the people we work with are passionate about what they do, as well as the technical decisions they make. Listen to the conversations in the coffee room or on Slack (a professional and organizational instant messenger program). People can be gleeful when they describe hacking up a quick fix to get something deployed. That glee isn't diminished if the quick fix causes technical debt that needs paying off in the future. The alternative is to have people who favor elegant solutions that solve problems with the fewest lines of code possible. These are the seeds of competing technical interests.

Example—The Seasoned Architect

A number of teams are adding a large enhancement to an existing product. An architect extended the architecture during the previous quarter. This was to make it easier for the addition of this enhancement. The architect is working from the team's design documents and has access to the code base. During implementation, the teams discover that the architecture isn't going to work. They express their concerns to the architect. The architect responds by saying, "If you did what I put in the design documentation, it would work fine."

The architect made technical decisions for the teams in the spirit of enablement. He thought doing so would make implementation easier. The problem is that these decisions happened too early, and in a vacuum. When faced with negative feedback, he was not receptive. His self-image was at risk. His interest was in getting the teams to follow his original design documentation—rather than in admitting a mistake or that the team had a reason for a new direction. The competing interests of emergent design and self-image can lead to failure. Delaying or avoiding feedback is dangerous.

Antipattern Antidotes

Here are some thoughts on how to resolve this antipattern:

- Commander's intent
    - Define the outcome of the work, so that everyone involved understands what needs to be accomplished. Make the definition clear and simple. This will establish guardrails for decision making as teams decide how to do the work.
- Level the playing field
    - Eliminate key-person risk by spreading the knowledge needed to make technical decisions. Don't hire the best

and brightest and then centralize decision making. Cutting the key person out of the process only generates employee retention risk. Allowing key-person risk to develop hurts people and teams. We have seen people misuse the political power they established through technical expertise. Their behavior was abysmal. Yet, the organization thought twice about parting ways with them. The message was crystal clear: "If you are a subject matter expert, your job is secure. No matter how much you misbehave." Work to level the playing field so that teams—not individuals—are the key technical contributors.

- Invest in automation
  - Embrace automated testing and continuous integration/continuous delivery. Do it for the entire development life cycle. It is one thing to tell another person that they made the wrong decision, but it's another thing when a machine tells a person that they made the wrong decision. There is still a place in the work environment for conversations and feedback; that is imperative to producing quality products. However, a failed automated test or a failed build has an air of credibility (and urgency).

PRODUCT INTERESTS

Feedback is critical for making decisions whether we are building an iOS application or an embedded software system. We need to know that our work is going to meet the needs of potential and existing customers. A common pattern for quick feedback in organizations is to get it from other employees. Product management is often the source for information from existing and potential customers. There is an expectation that they can provide valuable feedback.

Example—Product Manager Incentives

A number of teams are working on a product that serves many vertical industries (for example, healthcare, commercial, financial, and higher education). The team leader is anxious to prioritize the list of requests for the product. She wants her team to break the work down and get started. She calls a meeting with product managers in each vertical industry. The goal is a single prioritized list. She asks the product managers to come to the meeting knowing which features matter most.

When the meeting begins, the representative from higher education speaks first. He tells the group about a feature he would like to have added to the product for an existing customer. He draws a line in the sand, stating, "It's my highest priority." Other industry representatives take their turns identifying their highest priorities. The session's facilitator documents each feature on a whiteboard. After everyone has identified their top priority, it is clear that everyone's priority is different. The leader of the engineering team is at her wit's end about how to get to a single list since there is no overlap. A stalemate seems to be emerging. Then, one of the industry representatives announces that his vertical makes more revenue than the others. He then adds, "If we're here to make money, my request should be a higher priority."

Another industry representative chimes in. "My industry isn't the largest vertical. If you don't add our feature, we won't be able to sell the product to any new customers. No new sales means the sales team in this vertical won't be getting any commission, and neither will I."

This example shows another type of competing interest that can crop up in the middle level. These interests are outside the engineering teams' span of control. They are external to the teams doing the work, but they are not outside of the engineering teams' sphere of political interest. The product managers from each vertical industry are now in zero-sum territory. Features are being rank-ordered and only those at the top of the list are sure to get done. All of the representatives are coming to the table with the perspectives of their individual industries. They are also bringing their personal biases. No one is thinking of the whole product—or even the success of the entire company.

Antipattern Antidotes

Here are some thoughts on how to resolve this antipattern:

- Customer feedback is king
  - Stop playing the telephone game with internal employees, and talk to customers. Even internal applications are for someone to use. They are your customers.
  - When talking to customers is not possible, talk to close proxies. This includes salespeople and customer support personnel. Customer support is a rich source of feedback for internal and external applications.
  - Value feedback from people that use (or will use) the product over those outside of the value chain. Do not dismiss internal feedback.
- Understand financial incentives
  - Understand how people are financially incentivized. This is the first step in untangling competing product interests. This information is often closely guarded because compensation is usually the outcome of negotiation and bias. Knowledge at a macro level will suffice to help expose and defuse most work intake issues. For example, it is common for salespeople to get part of their compensation as a commission on sales. If the product is not meeting the needs of potential customers, the salesperson can't sell the product. Thus, no commission. This leads to salespeople having a huge incentive to inject work into the system. They want the product to meet the needs of those customers. Their compensation literally depends on it. Design your work intake process to highlight when work gets injected because of this.

PROCESS INTERESTS

There's no shortage of opinions about the processes that companies use to build products. From the C-level, all the way down to the team level, almost everyone has an opinion. Some feel that any hint of process is cumbersome; "We're agile, we don't need to follow any process!" Others have built careers out of creating and following processes.

Process opinions are often rooted in experiences that people had at other companies. Other sources include the internet, books, and conference presentations. It is hard to imagine that you have not heard statements like, "[Insert name of process] works for [insert name of big successful company], so why aren't we doing it?" How many firms have tried the *Spotify Model* because someone heard about it, watched a few YouTube videos, and thought it was cool?

A close partner of this particular type of competing interest is the *new-kid-on-the-block syndrome*. (Note: This is not related to the boy band.) This occurs when people take roles that influence their product's development path. The new people have a window of opportunity to make their names and have an impact on their products. Because they're new, they rarely have deep context about the current work in progress. They end up focusing on the thing they can see—the process to create products. Early opinions can miss some critical context. This context would be beneficial to solving root causes of product development challenges.

Example—Directing Your Own Fiefdom

The CEO agrees to an enterprise-sized chunk of work that is mission critical for the firm's largest customers. This is the kind of company-wide initiative that is so significant that it earns a code name. In this example, the code name is *Saturn*. When the initiative gets announced, everyone involved receives a mission patch to create team spirit. Saturn posters line the halls of the main office. Employees talk about Saturn in euphoric tones. When the work gets broken into smaller pieces for each area of the firm, that euphoria begins to sour.

The enterprise-sized chunk of work seemed to be well understood. However, it got decomposed for the three product development areas in the company. One department makes the front-end software, another department does the server-side development work, and a third department creates and manufactures the devices that the firm produces. Each department goes about doing its work in the way it has always been done. The enterprise-sized chunk of work is now three siloed development projects.

A few months after the departments started working on Saturn, the CEO asks for an update. The directors give the CEO updates that range from "It's going great" to "We haven't started yet." The data that has surfaced comes in different flavors. None of the directors are able to show meaningful progress. They cannot accurately forecast when their teams will complete the work.

In this example, each director's decision to operate in their own way has significant ramifications for the Saturn initiative. Each department's unique way of operating means the CEO isn't able to get a clear picture of how work is progressing. This kind of challenge results in things like process transformation initiatives, as well as changes in CIOs and CTOs.

Antipattern Antidotes

Here are some thoughts on how to resolve this antipattern:

- Diagram the process
  - Create a picture that shows the steps in the value delivery process. Use the picture to challenge why things happen in the order they do.
  - Simplify the process to remove handoffs or outside checkpoints.
- Understand the context
  - There's a story behind every process. It could be something like, "We hired a consultant and they told us to do this." It could also be, "We used to do it this way, missed something, and got sued by a customer." Understand the historical context behind why processes exist. It is imperative *before* changing them.

META ANTIDOTE

We explored competing interest antipattern antidotes throughout this chapter. It is important to remember that there is a meta antidote to these antipatterns. It is being explicit about the necessary outcome to meet the interests of the company. You must always ask, "Is this in the best interest of the company—or individuals?"

END-OF-CHAPTER QUESTIONS

Use the following to start a conversation about the contents of this chapter:

1. Describe any competing interests you have recently seen. How did these competing interests impact the team? How did they impact the work? How was the competing interest resolved?
2. What other middle management antipatterns have you seen? How did this pattern impact the people? How did it impact the work? How was it resolved?

25

WHEN WORK IS DONE

> **Learning Objectives**—by the end of this chapter, you will be able to:
> - ➤ Describe the concept of work acceptance
> - ➤ Recognize common work acceptance antipatterns

The majority of this book is about what to do when work has either arrived in your context or is already in progress. But what happens after it's done?

Let's face it—most software teams do not interface with customers. So how do they know that they have delivered what customers want? Delivery of value to customers will look different depending on your context. For example, Cloud-based software delivery might happen many times per day. Changes pass the continuous integration suite of tests and get deployed to production. If you are developing firmware for medical devices, delivery could be a given point during a year—for example, to coincide with a trade show. In both cases, there is some form of work acceptance. It might be a product owner on a Scrum team reviewing completed backlog items. It might also be an automated system verifying that changes did not wreak havoc. Acceptance is always a step in the value delivery process.

WORK ACCEPTANCE ANTIPATTERNS

"This Is the First Time I'm Seeing It."

We have worked with Scrum teams who heard this phrase during sprint reviews from the team's product owner. It was sometimes followed by, "and I like it." Other times, the comments that followed were not so positive.

The product owner is the embodiment of the agile principle, "Business people and developers must work together daily through the project." The product owner has a responsibility to represent business and customer needs to the Scrum team on a daily basis. If they are only showing up on sprint review day to see the output of the sprint, try these antipattern antidotes:

- Figure out how to get more of the product owner's time during the sprint. Commit to getting the person to attend X number of standups. If that is not possible, offer up the idea of a mid-sprint checkpoint. The product owner can see work that is done and offer their feedback. Delinquency is not a desired trait in a product owner.
- Build product owner acceptance into how the team operates. Do not save this step for sprint review; that is too late. Add a column to the team's board to make the rule explicit. The product owner's approval must happen before a backlog item is done.

"What Is This Acceptance You Speak Of?"

The word *acceptance* is a formal way of describing whether the enhancement or change is suitable. It is a deliberate feedback step that is often from the perspective of the customer or the business.

Gathering and reacting to feedback is part of being a professional. Yet, we have worked with teams who have no concept of acceptance. Developers write code, it gets tested and delivered, and the team moves on. In theory, this seems like a great self-directing team behavior. In practice, we have seen the lack of feedback come back and bite teams more often than not. The lack of a feedback loop can lead to doing the wrong thing—or the right thing in the wrong way. Lack of feedback also serves to promote the idea that the team is the expert on what needs to get done (and why). This type of thinking can cause teams to make products that leave customers confused.

If you see this antipattern, try these antipattern antidotes:

- Educate the stakeholders who you want to involve in the acceptance process about their role. Notify those stakeholders when you begin a piece of work that you will need their involvement in the acceptance process so that they will not be surprised later.
- Determine how to show the team that they need this type of feedback. Keep a running tally of how many completed items get rejected by customers or users.
- Determine who can give the team this type of feedback. If the team is a Scrum team, the product owner is the obvious person to deliver this type of feedback. If the team is doing something else, the person to offer this feedback might be less clear. The person giving feedback should have some sort of connection with the business and customers. Examples would include people from Sales, Marketing, Technical Support, and Product Management.

"Anyone Can Accept Any Item."

This is the polar opposite of the previous antipattern. In this scenario, anyone on the team can accept any item. This might work for some teams, but we have often seen this behavior promote the thinking that acceptance is checking the box. Or worse still—the standard for each team member to accept an item is not consistent. Some team members spend 30 seconds looking at items, while others spend 30 minutes.

A variation of this antipattern exists. The verbalized "anyone can accept any item" gets actualized as "I'm going to give my items to the same person to accept." This variation gets magnified when the entire team starts expecting one person to accept items, even though anyone can do it.

If you see this antipattern, try these antipattern antidotes:

- Create a checklist of steps to perform during acceptance. This ensures team members do it in a consistent way.
- Decide who will be involved in acceptance when you plan the work. This will allow everyone on the team to understand if a single person is being overloaded (or abused).
- Keep track of who is doing acceptance and make it visible. Ensure that the responsibility is being load balanced among team members.

END-OF-CHAPTER QUESTIONS

Use the following to start a conversation about the contents of this chapter:

1. Describe how work acceptance happens on your team. Was this something that the team agreed to, or did the wider organization mandate it?
2. What other work acceptance antipatterns have you seen? What did you do to resolve them?

Web Added Value™

This book has free material available for download from the
Web Added Value™ resource center at *www.jrosspub.com*

Section Four

Introspection

A WORK INTAKE CASE STUDY AS A BUSINESS NOVELLA, CHAPTER 4

It's been a week since the rough flow metrics discussion. James has realized that the idea of product development at Dandelion is more aspiration than reality. Much of the organization uses approaches from the late 1990s. The expectation of leadership is that strategic initiatives travel the happy path. They begin in the executive suite and are decomposed and slotted into business silos only to get reassembled—as if by magic—when everything is ready to deliver. It works . . . sometimes. Dandelion's success is because of product managers and product owners. They wrangle the disparate pieces of initiatives in the form of program management. As work crosses back and forth organizational boundaries, other work seeps into the pipeline. The flow distribution metrics that James shared across the management structure highlight the issue.

In a moment of dark reflection, James recalls the reactions after presenting the rough flow distribution and flow metrics. Hannah, the delivery manager for order systems, suggested that executives were out of touch with what it took to keep legacy systems running. If they wanted that much work done on the new product, Dandelion needed more hands-on keyboards and more Gantt charts. No one was sure if the Gantt chart thing was sarcasm. Sonja, one of the senior product owners, suggested renewed vigilance to stop work from jumping the queue. This work was being picked up by the team. She uttered her favorite Jocko Willink saying, "Discipline is the pathway to freedom." She was adamant that every team needed to understand its role in holding the line. It was as if everyone on the management committee was willing to throw someone else under the bus. It was disconcerting.

James and a small group strung together cycle-time data for a handful of epics that were ready to release across their whole value stream. Each of the epics traversed at least six organizational boundaries before getting close to done. At each step, the epic got reprioritized and resequenced. This was a huge clue to the flow problem. As the team put the final touches on the visualized flow, Ashish, one of the project managers from development, spoke up. He lamented that the handoffs between departments in IT were costing at least a month's delay. Every stop for reprioritization and resequencing was also an opportunity for something else to jump the queue.

James adjourned to The Annex for a bit of relaxation and . . . a team meeting. They decided to brainstorm possible solutions. The first batch of solutions represented attempts to solve the problem in one fell swoop. James's dad called this approach "praying for a five-run home run" (not a possibility). Most everyone agreed that pulling everyone involved in the new product into a single value chain—with one leader—would solve a ton of problems. The problem was that it would take forever to negotiate. There were lots of silos to undo, and no one enjoys mass reorganizations. The pain of reorganization outweighed the lack of evidence that streamlining flow would translate into more features in production. James needed some proof to match the theory and challenged the team to identify a few small-scale experiments to help sell the idea. They decided to give it some thought and meet again in the morning.

As the team gathered the next morning, James pulled Sonja to the side and asked what she thought of trying an experiment with a few of the teams she worked with. James's thought was to embed a database and test specialist in each of the teams. The teams would be much more self-contained. The people involved were all inside the IT department. This would reduce the number of executives involved. James's question was a seed.

Once everyone sat down with their morning caffeine, James shared a simple worksheet. The form had three columns: "Current State," "Desired Future State," and "How to Get There" (see Table S4.1). James opened the session. "I hope we can all agree that our mission is to find

Table S4.1   Future State

Current State	Desired Future State	How to Get There

a way to deliver the new product before someone else gets asked to do it. We can embrace that as our Commander's Intent (CI). I know that is a pretty straightforward statement, but does anyone disagree?" After there were head nods all around, James continued, "Let's see if we can identify three experiments that we can pull off to see if the changes could be effective at moving us closer to our goal."

Sonja opened the discussion. She suggested experimenting with self-contained teams to reduce handoffs. The seed James planted had germinated. Sonja even raised James's ante by adding a business analyst to each team's suggested mix.

Another suggestion was posting each team's monthly flow distribution and progress regarding the new product on the company's internal website. James spent the rest of the day socializing the ideas with the leadership committee. Even though there had been a few political tweaks, things were moving. Anna had provided her support for making change happen. "Let's do this and see what we learn," said Anna. "Standing around is not learning anything."

EXECUTING NEW IDEAS

This section culminates in a call to action. It is a call to begin changing the path that work takes when it enters your organization or team—to turn the phrase *work entry* into *work intake*. The process begins with awareness. Now it is your turn to put in the elbow grease. Unless you own the firm, you will probably have to make many small changes.

- **Step 1:** Consider the CI that guides your part of the organization. Can you answer how better work intake supports the CI? It is important to have this information in mind as your proverbial north star.
- **Step 2:** Reflect on the exercises at the ends of Sections One, Two, and Three. Consider what you have learned about work intake, where it enters, who is involved, and how you measure flow.

- **Step 3:** Brainstorm the parts of the current state that you want to change. Use the first two columns of Table S4.1 to capture:
  - Current State
    - What is currently happening?
  - Desired Future State
    - What do you want to happen?
- **Step 4:** Pick the idea you feel is the best starting point. Capture the steps and ideas needed to transform your reality—and one specific first step—in the *How to Get There* column of Table S4.1.
- **Step 5:** Get started!

AFTERWORD

Organizations exist to bring people together to achieve a common goal. As we noted at the beginning of this book, work intake is the largest determinant of whether an organization or team can get work done effectively. Organizations that are not effective find it difficult to meet their goals. We have attempted to give you the knowledge and tools needed to bring work intake under control. We are confident that you possess the tools to get started.

During the writing of this book, we presented this topic at conferences. We also spoke about this topic with friends, colleagues, and clients. None of them flinched when we described the premise of the book we were writing. This is because—to a person—they have seen this challenge before. They have lived through the pain. They understand and empathize.

Our journey with this topic started with small steps. A conversation turned into a blog entry. A blog entry turned into a podcast. Those were the seeds of this book. Those seeds blossomed into working versions of this material. Those early drafts spawned conference presentations. Those experiences have resulted in this volume.

—Thomas M. Cagley, Jr. and Jeremy Willets
Authors of *Mastering Work Intake: From Chaos to Predictable Delivery*

INDEX

Page numbers followed by "*f*" and "*t*" refer to figures and tables, respectively.